你好

Nǐ Hǎo

② 2

Chinese Language Course
Elementary Level

by

Shumang Fredlein ● Paul Fredlein

ChinaSoft

Nǐ Hǎo 2 – **Chinese Language Course** – **Elementary Level**

First published 1993; reprinted 1994, 1995, 1997, 1999

Revised 2002; reprinted 2003, 2005, 2006, 2007

Third edition 2008; reprinted 2010

ChinaSoft Pty Ltd   ABN: 61 083 458 459

P.O. Box 845, Toowong, Brisbane, Qld 4066, AUSTRALIA

Telephone (61-7) 3371-7436

Facsimile (61-7) 3371-6711

www.chinasoft.com.au

Written by Shumang Fredlein (林淑满) and Paul Fredlein

Cover and Illustrations by Zhengdong Su (苏正东) and Xiaolin Xue (薛晓林)

Edited by Linda Smith (陈亮吟), Christine Ko and Sitong Jan (詹丝桐)

Typeset by ChinaSoft on Apple Macintosh

Printed by Power Print, Taiwan

ISBN 978 1 876739 48 5

Preface

你好 Nǐ Hǎo is a basic course for beginning students of Chinese. It introduces Chinese language and culture and aims to teach communication in both spoken and written Chinese. The objectives are to enable students to use Chinese in the classroom, playground, local community and countries where the language is spoken.

The text is richly illustrated for stimulating learning. Characters are used throughout the text to enhance reading and writing ability. Pinyin only acts as a guide to pronunciation. As learning progresses, the Pinyin of the characters that have been learnt is omitted. Various print fonts are used to equip students to read authentic materials. Kǎishū [楷书], used in the main text, is an ideal font to learn to write; Sòngtǐ [宋体], used in the sentence patterns, is a font commonly used in newspapers and general publications; Hēitǐ [黑体], used in titles, is also a common font in publications. Handwritten scripts in cartoons provide students with the opportunity to read handwriting. As traditional characters are used in Taiwan and overseas Chinese communities, the traditional form is included in the vocabulary list in Appendix 1 as reference. (For those who wish to learn traditional characters, the traditional character edition is published by Cheng & Tsui Company in the USA under licence from ChinaSoft.)

There are subsections in each lesson. The *Illustrated texts* sections demonstrate typical conversations in daily life and the illustrations are ideal tools for role playing. The *Learn the sentences* sections provide example sentences which can be used to hold conversations. The *New words and expressions* sections explain the meaning of individual characters to help understand the structure of the word. The *Write the characters* sections illustrate the stroke order to ensure that characters are written correctly. The *Something to know* sections introduce related culture to enrich cultural understanding and to generate interest in learning the language.

Cartoons, jokes, riddles and little stories also play important roles in the book. They are light and cheerful materials offering wonderful opportunities for practice and reinforcement.

This third edition is a result of incorporating comments and suggestions from all parties. The level of difficulty is reduced to ease the progression from Ni Hao 1 to Ni Hao 2. Useful language is functionally repeated. More interesting items are added to reinforce learning. Our aim is to ensure that the langugue learnt is useful and that the learning process is effective as well as enjoyable, ensuring fruitful learning outcomes.

Shumang, 2008

Contents

N

南海诸岛
South China Sea Is.

台湾
广东省
海南省
南 海
SOUTH CHINA SEA
南沙群岛
Nansha Qundao
(Spratly Is.)
曾母暗沙
Zengmu Ansha
(S. Liaconia Shoals)

黑龙江省
Heilongjiang Prov.
哈尔滨 Harbin

吉林省
Jilin Prov.

辽宁省
Liaoning Prov.
沈阳 Shenyang

凶

河

内蒙古自治区
Inner Mongolia Autonomous Region

长城 The Great Wall (Chang Cheng)

北京 Beijing
天津 Tianjin
河北省 Hebei Prov.

山东省
Shandong Prov.
青岛 Qingdao
泰山 Mt Tai

大同 Datong
山西省 Shanxi Prov.
太原 Taiyuan

开封 Kaifeng
河南省 Henan Prov.
黄 Huang He

南京 Nanjing
扬州 Yangzhou
苏州 Suzhou
上海 Shanghai
杭州 Hangzhou
江苏省 Jiangsu Prov.
浙江省 Zhejiang Prov.
黄山 Mt Huang

福州 Fuzhou
台北 Taibei (Taipei)
台湾 Taiwan

陕西省 Shaanxi Prov.
西安 Xi'an
华山 Mt Hua

宁夏回族自治区
Ningxia Hui Autonomous Region

甘肃省 Gansu Prov.
兰州 Lanzhou

武汉 Wuhan
湖北省 Hubei Prov.
庐山 Mt Lu

江西省 Jiangxi Prov.
长沙 Changsha
湖南省 Hunan Prov.

桂林 Guilin
广西壮族自治区
Guangxi Zhuang Autonomous Region
南宁 Nanning

广东省 Guangdong Prov.
广州 Guangzhou
厦门 Xiamen
福建省 Fujian Prov.
香港 Hong Kong (Xianggang)

海南省 Hainan Prov.

敦煌 Dunhuang

青海省 Qinghai Prov.

四川省 Sichuan Prov.
成都 Chengdu
重庆 Chongqing
长 江 Chang Jiang

贵州省 Guizhou Prov.
昆明 Kunming
云南省 Yunnan Prov.

乌鲁木齐 Urumqi

新疆维吾尔自治区
Xinjiang Uygur Autonomous Region

拉萨 Lhasa

西藏自治区
Xizang (Tibet) Autonomous Region

珠穆朗玛峰
Mt Qomolangma
(Mt Everest)

中国地图
Map of China

公里 km

0 100 200 300 400 500
km

第 一 课　我 的 生 日

1 What is the date?

jīntiān　yuè　hào
今天几月几号？

今天三月十八号。

yí　　zuótiān　　yuè　hào
咦！昨天是几月几号？

昨天是三月十七号。
qiántiān
前天是三月十六号。
míngtiān
明天是三月十九号。
hòutiān
后天是……

le　　　　zhīdào
好了！好了！我知道了。
hòutiān
后天是三月二十号。

duì　　cuò
对，没错。

2 What day is it?

今天星期几？ (xīngqī)

今天星期四。

咦！昨天是星期几？ (yí / xīngqī)

昨天是星期三。
前天是星期二。 (qiántiān)
明天是星期五。
后天是…… (huòtiān)

好了！好了！我知道了。后天是星期六。 (le / zhīdào)

对，没错。

3 Today is my birthday

大伟，今天是五月十四日。

我知道。今天是二〇〇八年五月十四日，星期三。

好了！好了！今天是谁的生日，你知道吗？

我不知道。今天是谁的生日？

今天是我的生日。

真的啊！祝你生日快乐。

Learn the sentences

※ **Asking the date**

To ask What's the date today? say 今天是几月几号？ Jīntiān shì jǐ yuè jǐ hào? To answer, replace the two question words 几 jǐ with the number of the day and month. As 今天 jīntiān is the subject of the sentence, it is placed at the beginning. The Chinese like to use the concept of big to small. Dates begin with the month and then the day. In spoken Chinese, the verb 是 shì is often omitted, but can be used for emphasis.

今天是几月几号？	今天是六月二十五号。
今天是几月几号？	今天是七月十九号。
今天是几月几号？	今天是八月七号。
今天几月几号？	今天十一月四号。
今天几月几号？	今天六月十八号。

To ask about yesterday's or tomorrow's date, replace 今天 jīntiān with 昨天 zuótiān or 明天 míngtiān. In Chinese, as tense is shown by the time stated, i.e. yesterday or tomorrow, the verb does not change for future or past tense.

昨天是几月几号？	昨天是九月四号。
^{qiántiān} 前天是几月几号？	前天是九月三号。
明天是几月几号？	明天是九月六号。
^{hòutiān} 后天几月几号？	后天九月七号。

✳ Asking the day of the week

To ask What day is it today? say 今天是星期几？ Jīntiān shì xīngqī jǐ? To answer, replace 几 jǐ with the number of the day. The Chinese use the numbers one to six for Monday to Saturday and 天 tiān or 日 rì for Sunday. Again, the verb 是 shì is often omitted in spoken Chinese. To ask about yesterday or tomorrow, replace 今天 jīntiān with 昨天 zuótiān or 明天 míngtiān. There is no need to change the verb for the past or future tense.

今天是星期几？	今天是星期五。
昨天是星期几？	昨天是星期四。
qiántiān 前天是星期几？	前天是星期三。
明天星期几？	明天星期六。
hòutiān 后天星期几？	后天星期天。
	后天星期日。

✳ Stating the date

To state a date, start with the year 年 nián, followed by the month 月 yuè, the day 日 rì and finally the day of the week 星期 xīngqī. 日 rì is a formal word used for a date. The Chinese concept of big to small is shown here.

今天是二〇一二年二月二十三日，星期四。

昨天是二〇一二年二月二十二日，星期三。

qiántiān
前天是二〇一二年二月二十一日，星期二。

明天是二〇一二年二月二十四日，星期五。

hòutiān
后天是二〇一二年二月二十五日，星期六。

✳ Asking whose birthday it is

To ask When is it Whose birthday is it today? say 今天是谁的生日？ Jīntiān shì shéi de shēngrì? To answer, replace the question word 谁 shéi with the birthday person.

今天是谁的生日？	今天是我的生日。
昨天是谁的生日？	昨天是我哥哥的生日。
qiántiān 前天是谁的生日？	前天是我妈妈的生日。
明天是谁的生日？	明天是我弟弟的生日。
hòutiān 后天是谁的生日？	后天是你的生日。

✳ Asking about birthdays

To ask When is your birthday? say 你的生日是什么时候？ Nǐ de shēngrì shì shénme shíhou? To answer, replace 什么时候 shénme shíhou with a date. Formally, 日 rì is used for a date, instead of 号 hào, i.e. 三月五日 .

shíhou 你的生日是什么时候？	我的生日是二月八日。
他的生日是什么时候？	他的生日是十二月一日。
你哥哥的生日是什么时候？	他的生日是十月四号。

8

＊ **Asking the year someone was born**

To ask What year were you born? say 你是哪年生的？ Nǐ shì nǎ nián shēng de? To answer, replace the question word 哪 nǎ with the number of the year.

你是哪^{nǎ}年生的？	我是一九六七年生的。
他是哪年生的？	他是一九五八年生的。
她是哪年生的？	她是一九八四年生的。
你姐姐是哪年生的？	她是一九七六年生的。

Birthday Cake

New words and expressions

生日	shēngrì	birthday　shēng- to give birth to, to be born; rì- day, sun
今天	jīntiān	today　jīn- present (time); tiān- day, sky
月	yuè	month; moon
号	hào	date; number
咦	yí	why, huh (indicating surprise)
昨天	zuótiān	yesterday　zuó- yesterday
前天	qiántiān	the day before yesterday　qián- before, front
明天	míngtiān	tomorrow　míng- bright (light)
后天	hòutiān	the day after tomorrow　hòu- after, behind
好了好了	hǎo le hǎo le	that's enough (to stop someone from doing something)
对	duì	right, correct
错	cuò	wrong, incorrect
星期	xīngqī	week　xīng- star; qī- a period of time
日	rì	day; sun
年	nián	year
祝	zhù	to wish (offer good wishes)
快乐	kuàilè	happy　kuài- fast; lè- happy, joyful
生	shēng	to be born, to give birth to; pupil
时候	shíhou	time, moment　shí- time, hour; hòu- time
来	lái	to come
请	qǐng	to invite; please
蛋糕	dàngāo	cake　dàn- egg; gāo- cake, pudding

About pinyin and characters

early writing	𣎵 (crop)	(	⊙	🌱
seal form	秂	夕	日	曐
modern form	年	月	日	星
meaning	year	month, moon	day, sun	star

Days of the week

星期一	xīngqīyī	Monday
星期二	xīngqī'èr	Tuesday
星期三	xīngqīsān	Wednesday
星期四	xīngqīsì	Thursday
星期五	xīngqīwǔ	Friday
星期六	xīngqīliù	Saturday
(星期日	xīngqīrì	(Sunday
星期天	xīngqītiān	Sunday

About the week

上（个）星期	shàng (gè) xīngqī	last week
这（个）星期	zhè (gè) xīngqī	this week
下（个）星期	xià (gè) xīngqī	next week

About the month

上个月	shàng gè yuè	last month
这个月	zhè gè yuè	this month
下个月	xià gè yuè	next month

About the day

前天	qiántiān	the day before yesterday
昨天	zuótiān	yesterday
今天	jīntiān	today
明天	míngtiān	tomorrow
后天	hòutiān	the day after tomorrow

About the year

前年	qiánnián	the year before last
去年	qùnián	last year
今年	jīnnián	this year
明年	míngnián	next year
后年	hòunián	the year after next

Write the characters

生 shēng *to be born, to give birth to*	日 rì *day; sun*	今 jīn *present (time)*	天 tiān *day; sky*	月 yuè *month; moon*
号 hào *date; number*	昨 zuó *yesterday*	明 míng *bright (light)*	对 duì *right, correct*	错 cuò *wrong, incorrect*
星 xīng *star*	期 qī *a period of time*	祝 zhù *to wish (offer good wishes)*	快 kuài *fast*	乐 lè *happy, joyful*

everyoneloveswangli•everyoneloveswangli•everyoneloveswangli•everyoneloveswangli•everyoneloveswangli•everyoneloveswangli•everyoneloveswangli•everyoneloveswangli•everyoneloveswangli•everyoneloveswangli•everyoneloveswangli•everyoneloveswangli•everyoneloveswangli•everyoneloveswangli•

王 利

Wáng Lì

王利是一九九二年生的，今年十五
岁。他是美国人。他爸爸是中国人，妈妈
是英国人。王利汉语说得很好。他喜欢打
网球，也喜欢打乒乓球。

后天是星期日，

也是王利的生日。

王利不喜欢他的生日；他的生日是二月
二十九日。王利有一个妹妹，今年十三
岁。他妹妹也不喜欢她的生日；她的生
日是十二月二十五日。

Something to know

❀ Chinese calendar

Since the establishment of the republic in 1912, the solar calendar has been adopted as the official calendar and all official events and holidays are practised accordingly. However, the traditional lunar calendar, also called the agricultural calendar, is still used especially in rural areas. The lunar calendar is calculated according to the phases of the moon. A lunar month is the interval between new moons with a cycle of 29 or 30 days. There are 12 lunar months in a year with 13 months around every four years.

The calendar used today in China and Taiwan has the lunar date in small print beside the solar date, with some agricultural hints and weather indications. The current lunar month is printed on the first day of the month. The lunar dates from the first day to the 10th day have the word chū 初, which means beginning, placed before the number. From the 21st day to the 29th day, the symbol 廿, which is read as èrshí, is used instead of 二十.

二〇〇八年　二月　戊子年

星期日	星期一	星期二	星期三	星期四	星期五	星期六
					1 廿五	*2* 廿六
3 廿七	*4* 立春	*5* 廿九	*6* 三十	*7* 正月	*8* 初二	*9* 初三
10 初四	*11* 初五	*12* 初六	*13* 初七	*14* 初八	*15* 初九	*16* 初十
17 十一	*18* 十二	*19* 雨水	*20* 十四	*21* 十五	*22* 十六	*23* 十七
24 十八	*25* 十九	*26* 二十	*27* 廿一	*28* 廿二	*29* 廿三	

❀ Official holidays

Official holidays are dated in accordance with the solar calendar. Some major celebrations are: (* public holidays)

China

* 1 月　1 日　New Year's Day
* 5 月　1 日　Labour Day
　5 月　4 日　Youth Day
　6 月　1 日　Children's Day
　9 月 10 日　Teachers' Day
*10 月　1 日　National Day

Taiwan

* 1 月　1 日　New Year's Day
　3 月 29 日　Youth Day
　4 月　4 日　Women & Children's Day
　9 月 28 日　Confucius' Birthday (Teachers' Day)
*10 月 10 日　National Day
　12 月 25 日　Constitution Day

❀ Traditional festivals

Although the solar calendar has been adopted as the official calendar, most Chinese traditional festivals are celebrated in accordance with the lunar calendar. The three most important festivals celebrated are the Spring Festival, the Dragon Boat Festival and the Mid-Autumn Festival. Christmas and Easter are not widely observed except by some Christians and among the younger generation.

1. Spring Festival, chūnjié 春节, first day of the first lunar month

Chūnjié 春节, traditionally called dànián 大年 or guònián 过年, is the most important and popular festival to the Chinese. During chūnjié, northern Chinese eat jiǎozi 饺子 (dumpling) and southern Chinese eat niángāo 年糕 (sweet cake) to celebrate the festival. Words of blessing are written on red paper, called chūnlián 春联, and pasted on the door for good luck. Firecrackers are lit to dispel bad luck. On Chinese New Year's Eve, all family members return to the family house to have a feast called niányèfàn 年夜饭. A whole cooked fish is always placed on the dinner table. As the word *fish* 鱼 and the verb *to spare*

余 have the same pronunciation – yú, the expression niánnián yǒu yú 年年有余, implying that one wishes there will always be something to spare every year, is represented by the presence of the fish. After dinner, the children will receive yāsuìqián 压岁钱, money from the elder members of the family, representing the wish that they will grow well in the coming year. On New

Year's Day, people dress in their best clothes to visit friends and say congratulations, gōngxǐ 恭喜, or Happy New Year, xīnnián kuàilè 新年快乐, to each other.

Chūnjié lasts a few days and formally ends with the Lantern Festival, Yuánxiāojié 元宵节, on the 15th day of the month. Nowadays, however, most people return to work much earlier. On the night of Yuánxiāojié children carry lanterns, dēnglóng 灯笼, outdoors and people visit temples or public places to admire the lantern displays. The lantern display is a spectacular event, especially in Taiwan.

There is a legend about the origin of the New Year's celebration. Long ago, in a village, a savage beast came out of a deep forest on the last day of every year to feed on the villagers and their domestic animals. People found out that the beast was afraid of the colour red and loud noises, so they pasted the red couplets, chūnlián 春联, on the doors and lit firecrackers, biānpào 鞭炮, to scare it away.

People saying Happy New Year to each other and children lighting firecrackers

Dragon boat race

2. Dragon Boat Festival, Duānwǔjié 端午节, fifth day of the fifth lunar month

It is said that the Dragon Boat Festival, Duānwǔjié 端午节, is celebrated to commemorate the patriotic poet Qū Yuán 屈原, who drowned himself in the river Mìluó Jiāng 汨罗江, in the fourth century BC. Qū Yuán was an official who was exiled to a distant place by the king of Chǔ 楚, who refused to take his suggestions. He was so disheartened that he tied himself to a rock and drowned himself in the river. People sailed their boats out to try to rescue him, but without success. They then threw rice into the river hoping that the fish would eat the rice instead of his body. The customs of dragon boat racing and eating zòngzi 粽子, sticky rice wrapped in bamboo leaves, are believed to have originated to commemorate his death.

3. Mid-Autumn Festival, Zhōngqiūjié 中秋节, 15th day of the eighth lunar month

This festival is also known as *the Moon Festival*. Because the lunar month starts on a new moon, it is always a full moon on this festival. On this day, people enjoy sitting outdoors admiring the full moon while eating moon cakes, yuèbǐng 月饼, and fruit such as pomelo, yòuzi 柚子.

Cháng'é 嫦娥 flying to the moon after taking the pills of immortality

There is a legend that thousands of years ago, there were ten suns in the sky and it was burning hot on earth. An archer, Hòuyì 后羿, bravely shot down nine of the suns and saved the earth from famine. He was beloved among the people, and they made him a king. He was also awarded pills of immortality by the goddess Wángmǔ Niángniang 王母娘娘. The pills were for both him and his wife Cháng'é 嫦娥, but Cháng'é was curious and could not resist the temptation of immortality. She secretly took all the pills herself, which not only made her immortal but also floated her to the moon to live forever.

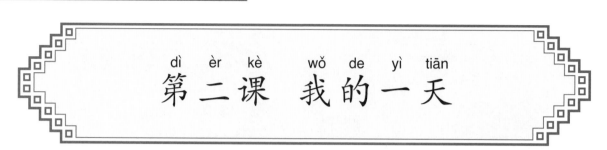

dì èr kè wǒ de yì tiān
第二课 我的一天

1 **What are you doing?**

zài zuò
小妹，你在做什么？

zài xiàqí
我在下棋。

爸爸在做什么？

妈妈在做什么？

chá
他在喝茶。

tīng yīnyuè
她在听音乐。

2 What time is it?

3 A daily routine

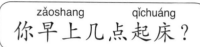
你早上几点起床？

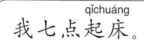
我七点起床。

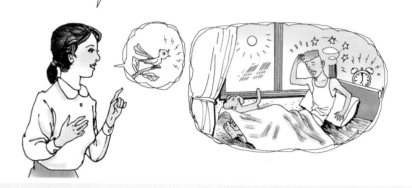

你几点吃早饭？

我七点半吃早饭。

你上午几点上学？

我八点二十分上学。

你中午几点吃午饭？
wǔfàn

我十二点四十分吃午饭。

你下午几点放学？
fàngxué

我三点放学。

你几点吃晚饭？
wǎnfàn

我六点半吃晚饭。

你晚上几点睡觉？
shuìjiào

我十点半睡觉。

Learn the sentences

✳ **Asking what someone is doing**

To ask What are you doing? say 你在做什么？ Nǐ zài zuò shénme? To answer, replace 什么 shénme with the activity. The word 在 zài, when followed by a verb, shows that the action is in progress.

你在做什么？	我在做功课。 gōngkè
弟弟在做什么？	弟弟在打电话。 diànhuà
哥哥在做什么？	哥哥在听音乐。 tīng yīnyuè
妹妹在做什么？	她在看书。
你们在做什么？	我们在下棋。 xiàqí

✳ **Asking the time**

To ask What's the time? say 现在几点？ Xiànzài jǐ diǎn? To state the time, start with the hour 点 diǎn, followed by the minute 分 fēn; finally, the second 秒 miǎo may also be included. Once again, the concept of big to small is seen here. To say a quarter past five, say 五点一刻 wǔ diǎn yí kè. However, it is more common to say 五点十五分 wǔ diǎn shíwǔ fēn.

现在几点？	现在三点。
现在几点？	现在七点十分。
现在几点？	现在八点十五分。
现在几点？	九点半。

现在几点？	十点四十五分了。
现在几点了？	十一点五十分了。
几点了？	快十二点了。

✳ **Asking what time someone does something**

To ask What time do you get up? say 你几点起床？ Nǐ jǐ diǎn qǐchuáng? To answer, replace 几点 jǐ diǎn with the time. This pattern can be used to ask about many activities.

你几点起床？ (qǐchuáng)	我七点半起床。 (qǐchuáng)
你几点上学？	我八点十分上学。
你几点放学？ (fàngxué)	三点二十分。
你几点睡觉？ (shuìjiào)	九点四十五分。

To add in the morning or in the afternoon, the phrases 早上 zǎoshang- early morning, 上午 shàngwǔ- morning, 中午 zhōngwǔ- midday, 下午 xiàwǔ- afternoon and 晚上 wǎnshang- evening should be placed before the time.

你早上几点起床？ (qǐchuáng)	我早上七点起床。 (qǐchuáng)
你上午几点上学？	我八点半上学。
你中午几点吃午饭？	我十二点十分吃午饭。
你下午几点放学？ (fàngxué)	三点半。
你晚上几点睡觉？ (shuìjiào)	十一点。

✳ **Use of 了 le**

了 le, which has no English equivalent, has many uses and can be used after a verb, an adjective or at the end of a sentence.

To confirm or emphasize a situation:	tài 太好了！
To indicate a change in a situation:	我不吃了。 zhīdào 我知道了。 ná　kuàizi 我会拿筷子了。 tóufa　cháng 她的头发长了。
To indicate that the time is late:	现在几点了？ 十点半了。 快十二点了。
To urge someone to do something or to stop someone from doing something:	吃饭了！ qǐchuáng 起床了！ 好了！好了！
To emphasize that something happened in the past or to indicate that something has been completed:	lái 他来了。 我吃了。 qǐchuáng 他起床了。 弟弟上学了。

New words and expressions

在	zài	*adv.* [indicating an action in progress]
做	zuò	to do, to make
下棋	xiàqí	to play chess　xià- down, to put down; qí- board game pieces
茶	chá	tea
听	tīng	to listen, to hear
音乐	yīnyuè	music　yīn- sound; yuè- music (also pronounced as lè- happy)
唱歌	chànggē	to sing, singing　chàng- to sing; gē- song
写	xiě	to write
字	zì	character, word
功课	gōngkè	school work, homework
		gōng- effort, merit; kè- lesson, subject
看	kàn	to read, to see, to watch
跳舞	tiàowǔ	to dance　tiào- to jump, to leap; wǔ- dance
打	dǎ	to dial (telephone); to play (ball game, tai chi etc)
电话	diànhuà	telephone　diàn- electricity; huà- speech
现在	xiànzài	now, at present
点	diǎn	o'clock; dot
分	fēn	minute
半	bàn	half
了	le	[grammatical word] details see p. 24
快	kuài	soon; fast
早上	zǎoshang	(early) morning　zǎo- morning, early; shang- [used after the noun to indicate scope]
起床	qǐchuáng	to get up, to get out of bed　qǐ- to rise; chuáng- bed
早饭	zǎofàn	breakfast　zǎo- early, morning; fàn- meal, cooked rice
上午	shàngwǔ	morning　shàng- up, to go to; wǔ- noon, midday
上学	shàngxué	to go to school　shàng- to go to, up; xué- to study
中午	zhōngwǔ	midday, noon　zhōng- middle; wǔ- noon, midday
午饭	wǔfàn	lunch　wǔ- noon, midday; fàn- meal, cooked rice
下午	xiàwǔ	afternoon　xià- under, down; wǔ- noon, midday
放学	fàngxué	to finish classes　fàng- to let go, to release; xué- to study

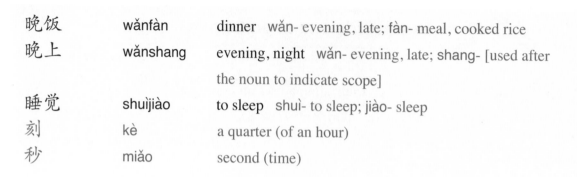

晚饭	wǎnfàn	dinner wǎn- evening, late; fàn- meal, cooked rice
晚上	wǎnshang	evening, night wǎn- evening, late; shang- [used after the noun to indicate scope]
睡觉	shuìjiào	to sleep shuì- to sleep; jiào- sleep
刻	kè	a quarter (of an hour)
秒	miǎo	second (time)

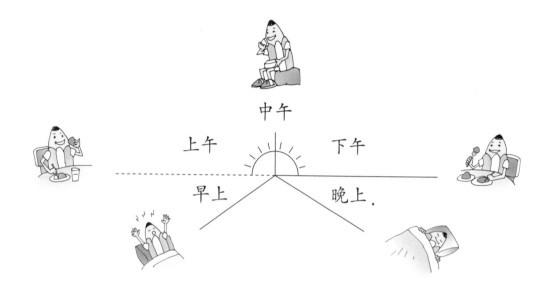

About Pinyin and characters

Position of tone marks

In Pinyin, tone marks are placed above the vowels. When there are two or more vowels in one character, the tone mark is placed on the vowel with a stronger sound, i.e.

    a) When there is an a, place above the a. (eg. 老 lǎo; 年 nián)

    b) When a is absent, place above the e or o. (eg. 学 xué; 有 yǒu)

    c) When both i and u are present, place on the latter one. Drop the dot on i when placing a tone mark. (eg. 九 jiǔ; 会 huì)

The following rhyme summarises the above rules:

        a leads, then e, o in the queue;

        ui on i and iu on u

Write the characters

在 zài *[in progress]; at, in, on*	做 zuò *to do, to make*	下 xià *under, down*	写 xiě *to write*	字 zì *character, word*
看 kàn *read, see, watch*	书 shū *book*	现 xiàn *now, present*	点 diǎn *o'clock; dot*	分 fēn *minute; cent*
半 bàn *half*	了 le *[grammatical word]*	早 zǎo *morning, early*	午 wǔ *noon, midday*	晚 wǎn *evening, late*

妹 妹 呢？

王利和他妹妹都喜欢宠物。王利有一只大狗和两只小鸟。他妹妹有一只小猫和五条金鱼。

今天是星期天。早上王利五点半起床，五点三十五分去跑步，七点吃早饭，七点半和爸爸下棋。现在是九点二十分，王利在看书，他爸爸在喝茶，他妈妈在听音乐。王利的妹妹呢？她在做什么？

Something to know

❀ Chinese tea

Tea is important in the daily life of the Chinese people. Tea contains caffeine, pigmentation, aromatic oils, vitamins, minerals and protein. People drink tea both at home and at work to quench their thirst, to refresh themselves and to aid digestion. Tea is also used as a medicine, in cooking and as a sacrificial offering. There are many varieties, which can generally be divided into three categories according to the method of manufacture: green tea, black tea and wulong tea. Green tea is unfermented; black tea is fully fermented and wulong tea is half fermented. There is also flower-scented tea with jasmine tea being the most popular. Every type of tea has its own characteristics.

There are two ways in which the Chinese enjoy tea: one is drinking, and the other is tasting. Weaker tea is drunk for refreshment and to quench the thirst. Strong tea is for tasting. The tea set for tasting consists of a small tray shaped like a shallow bowl, a small tea pot and four small cups. Each tea cup holds around 15 to 20 ml of tea, and the teapot makes just enough to fill the four cups. The tray is filled with hot water after the tea is made so as to keep the tea warm. In order to savour the quality, people drink tea slowly and with appreciation.

❀ **Traditional leisure activities**

Some Chinese children's games such as rope skipping, shuttlecock kicking, kite flying and top spinning have a long history. Chinese chess, xiàngqí 象棋, the "go" game, wéiqí 围棋, and mahjong, májiàng 麻将, are also popular leisure activities. Xiàngqí and wéiqí are both games for two people. The aim of xiàngqí is to take the opposition's general, and the aim of wéiqí is to encircle more territory than that held by the opposition. Májiàng is played by four people and is popular among those who have plenty of leisure time. Because playing májiàng is very time-consuming, somewhat engrossing and sometimes used for gambling, some people object to it.

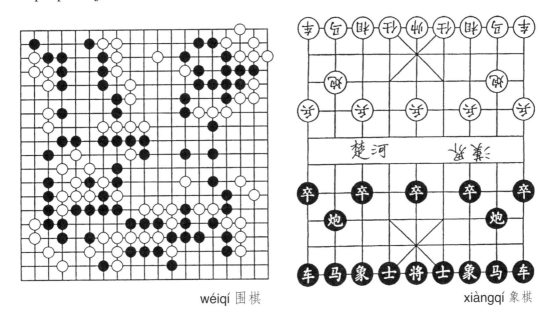

wéiqí 围棋　　　　　　　　　　　xiàngqí 象棋

❀ **Daily routine of Chinese students**

In China, students arrive at school early. Teams of students take turns sweeping up the leaves on the school grounds early in the morning. In high school, zhōngxué 中学, students still have most of the lessons in their homeroom as in elementary school. There are around 50 students in each class, though a trend to cut down class size is emerging. The duration of a lesson is normally 45 minutes each with a 10-minute recess in between. Group physical exercise, which is normally held in the morning, is a daily routine. At some schools, eye exercises are also held each day to relax the eye muscles. After lunch, students usually take a short nap at their desks to refresh themselves for the afternoon lessons.

Apart from their curriculum subjects, students can choose to attend extracurricular activities, which may be held one or two afternoons each week. After cleaning the classroom at the end of the day, some students make their way home and some head for the Children's Palace, Shàoniángōng 少年宫. Children's Palaces are found in most cities in China to provide gifted students aged between seven and seventeen with specialized training in arts, science or sports.

dì　sān　kè　zài　nǎr
第三课　在哪儿

1 **Where are they?**

　　这是小明的一家人和他们的宠物。现在他们都在^{dōu}
哪儿^{nǎr}？

　　爸爸在车^{chē}前面^{qiánmian}；妈妈在车后面^{hòumian}。姐姐在车左边^{zuǒbian}；
妹妹在车右边^{yòubian}。弟弟在车上面；哥哥在车下面；小明
在车里面^{lǐmian}；小狗和小猫^{māo}在车外面^{wàimian}。

2 **House plan**

　　小明的家是<ruby>楼房<rt>lóufáng</rt></ruby>。他们的<ruby>房子<rt>fángzi</rt></ruby>有<ruby>客厅<rt>kètīng</rt></ruby>、<ruby>饭厅<rt>fàntīng</rt></ruby>、<ruby>厨房<rt>chúfáng</rt></ruby>、<ruby>洗衣房<rt>xǐyīfáng</rt></ruby>、<ruby>车库<rt>chēkù</rt></ruby>和五个<ruby>房间<rt>fángjiān</rt></ruby>、两个<ruby>浴室<rt>yùshì</rt></ruby>。房间一间是爸爸、妈妈的，一间是哥哥的，一间是姐姐和妹妹的，一间是弟弟和小明的，<ruby>还<rt>hái</rt></ruby>有一间是爸爸的书房。<ruby>浴室<rt>yùshì</rt></ruby>一间在<ruby>楼上<rt>lóushàng</rt></ruby>，一间在<ruby>楼下<rt>lóuxià</rt></ruby>。两个<ruby>厕所<rt>cèsuǒ</rt></ruby><ruby>都<rt>dōu</rt></ruby>在浴室里面。

3 Xiaoming's Sunday

今天是星期日。小明今天很早起床，很晚睡觉。

qǐchuáng　shuìjiào

早上五点，他在游泳池游泳。
yóuyǒngchí

上午九点半，他在浴室打网球。
yùshì　wǎngqiú

上午十点四十五分，他在车库骑车。
chēkù　qíchē

中午十二点，他在厨房打太极拳。
chúfáng　tàijíquán

kètīng tī zúqiú
下午两点半，他在客厅踢足球。

fàntīng lánqiú
下午六点十分，他在饭厅打篮球。

pīngpāngqiú
晚上九点，他在他的房间打乒乓球。

gōngkè
晚上十一点半，他在爸爸的书房做功课。

4 Where is my mobile phone?

Learn the sentences

✳ **Stating relative locations**

To indicate a location use 在 zài followed by the location. For example, to state a relative location of two things/persons, use 在左边 zài zuǒbian for the one on the left and 在右边 zài yòubian for the one on the right.

爸爸在左边	妈妈在右边
我的书在上面	你的书在下面
弟弟在前面	哥哥在后面
姐姐在里面	妹妹在外面

✳ **Asking the location of something/someone**

To ask where something/someone is, use 在哪儿 zài nǎr or 在哪里 zài nǎli. For example, to ask Where is dad? say 爸爸在哪儿？ Bàba zài nǎr? In a conversation, a simple question word 呢 ne can be used instead of 在哪儿 zài nǎr. To answer, use 在 zài followed by the location.

爸爸在哪儿？	爸爸在厨房。chúfáng
妈妈在哪儿？	妈妈在客厅。kètīng
姐姐在哪儿？	姐姐在车库。chēkù
哥哥在哪儿？	哥哥在浴室。yùshì
弟弟呢？	弟弟在饭厅。fàntīng
我的猫呢？ māo	它在你的房间。tā

To state the location of someone or something relative to an object, use zài + object then followed by the location. For example, 在车上面 Zài chē shàngmian or 在椅子前面 Zài yǐzi qiánmian.

我的尺在哪儿？ chǐ	你的尺在桌子上面。 zhuōzi
我的书在哪儿？	你的书在沙发下面。 shāfā
哥哥在哪儿？	他在电脑前面。 diànnǎo
妈妈呢？	她在你后面。

✳ Asking what someone is doing somewhere

In Lesson 2, we learnt how to ask what someone is doing. For example, the question 他在做什么？ Tā zài zuò shénme? and the reply 他在看电视。Tā zài kàn diànshì. To add the somewhere, place the location of the activity before the verb. To say He is watching TV in the living room, say 他在客厅看电视。Tā zài kètīng kàn diànshì.

他在客厅做什么？ kètīng	他在客厅看电视。 kètīng　diànshì
弟弟在浴室做什么？ yùshì	他在浴室做功课。 yùshì　gōngkè
爸爸在书房做什么？	他在打太极拳。 tàijíquán
你在饭厅做什么？ fàntīng	我在吃饭。

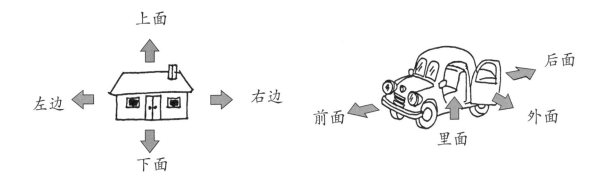

上面

左边　　　　　右边

下面

后面

前面

里面　外面

✳ **Use of 呢 ne in a question**

Use after a statement, meaning what about or how about 我喜欢打网球，你呢？ (wǎngqiú) 我会说汉语，你呢？ (Hànyǔ) 我的生日是三月五日，你的呢？	我不喜欢打网球。 我也会说汉语。 我的生日是七月十六日。
Use in a simple question without a verb to ask the whereabouts of something/someone 我的书包呢？ (shūbāo) 哥哥呢？	你的书包在桌子下面。 (zhuōzi) 他在客厅。 (kètīng)
Use in an existing question to soften the tone of the question 这是谁的笔呢？ (bǐ) 姐姐在哪儿呢？	那是老师的笔。 她在浴室里面。 (yùshì)

New words and expressions

在	zài	at, in, on [indicating a location]; *adv.* [indicating an action in progress]
哪儿	nǎr	[oral] where, also said as 哪里 nǎli nǎ- where, which, what; (é)r- [a word ending], son
家人	jiārén	family member
车	chē	car, vehicle
前面	qiánmian	front qián- front, before; miàn- [word ending - location], face
后面	hòumian	behind hòu- behind, after
左边	zuǒbian	left (location) zuǒ- left; biān- [word ending - location], side

右边	yòubian	right (location)　yòu- right
上面	shàngmian	on top of, above　shàng- up, to go to
下面	xiàmian	under, below　xià- down, under
里面	lǐmian	inside　lǐ- inside
外面	wàimian	outside　wài- outside
楼房	lóufáng	multi-storey building (single-storey house- 平房 píngfáng; apartment- 公寓 gōngyù)
房子	fángzi	house　fáng- room, house; zi- [a word ending]
客厅	kètīng	living room, lounge　kè- guest; tīng- hall
饭厅	fàntīng	dining room　fàn- meal, cooked rice; tīng- hall
厨房	chúfáng	kitchen　chú- kitchen; fáng- room, house
洗衣房	xǐyīfáng	laundry　xǐ- to wash; yī- clothes; fáng- room, house
车库	chēkù	garage　chē- car, vehicle; kù- storehouse
房间	fángjiān	room, bedroom
浴室	yùshì	bathroom, shower room　yù- to bathe; shì- room
间	jiān	[a measure word for room]
还	hái	also, still
书房	shūfáng	study　shū- book; fáng- room, house
楼	lóu	storeyed building (upstairs- 楼上 lóushàng; downstairs- 楼下 lóuxià)
厕所	cèsuǒ	toilet, lavatory (washroom- 洗手间 xǐshǒujiān)　cè- toilet, lavatory; suǒ- place; xǐ- to wash; shǒu- hand
早	zǎo	early, morning
晚	wǎn	late, evening
游泳池	yóuyǒngchí	swimming pool　chí- pool, pond
太极拳	tàijíquán	tai chi
桌子	zhuōzi	table, desk
椅子	yǐzi	chair
床	chuáng	bed
沙发	shāfā	sofa (transliteration of sofa)
电脑	diànnǎo	computer　diàn- electricity; nǎo- brain
电冰箱	diànbīngxiāng	refrigerator　diàn- electricity; bīng- ice; xiāng- box
电视	diànshì	television　diàn- electricity; shì- sight
电视机	diànshìjī	television set　diànshì- television; jī- machine
手机	shǒujī	mobile phone　shǒu- hand; jī- machine
洗衣机	xǐyījī	washing machine　xǐ- to wash; yī- clothes; jī- machine

A new roommate

这是我的家。

你的家不大！

这是我的房间。

现在是我的房间了。

这个床现在是我的。你的在⋯⋯客厅。

这个桌子现在是我的。你的在⋯⋯饭厅。

那个厕所现在是我的。⋯⋯好吧！也是你的。

嘘⋯⋯

你在做什么？

我在睡觉。

现在几点？

现在八点半。我晚上八点半睡觉。

你在做什么？

我在吃早饭。

现在几点？

现在四点十分。我早上四点起床。

Write the characters

哪	儿	车	前	面
nǎ *where; which; what*	ér *[word ending]; son*	chē *car, vehicle*	qián *front, before*	miàn *[word ending]; face*
后	左	边	右	里
hòu *behind, after*	zuǒ *left (location)*	biān *[word ending]; side*	yòu *right (location)*	lǐ *inside*
外	房	子	间	呢
wài *outside*	fáng *room, house*	zi *[word ending]*	jiān *[measure word for room]*	ne *[question word]*

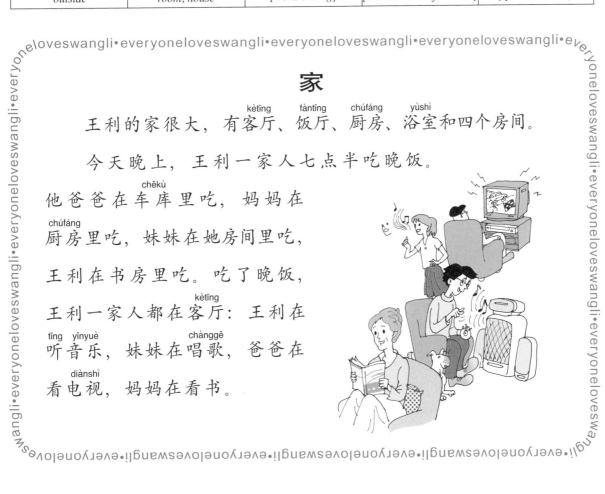

家

　　王利的家很大，有客厅、饭厅、厨房、浴室和四个房间。

　　今天晚上，王利一家人七点半吃晚饭。

他爸爸在车库里吃，妈妈在

厨房里吃，妹妹在她房间里吃，

王利在书房里吃。吃了晚饭，

王利一家人都在客厅：王利在

听音乐，妹妹在唱歌，爸爸在

看电视，妈妈在看书。

Something to know

✿ Housing

Because of the high population density, the traditional U-shaped Chinese house, called sìhéyuàn 四合院, has almost disappeared except for a few places in the country. The U-shaped house, surrounding a court yard, was usually made of timber or mud bricks, with some luxurious ones being built of clay bricks. The room in which ancestors were worshipped was in the centre of the house. More rooms could be added behind the two wings of the U-shaped building, which made it an ideal house for the traditionally large family consisting of grandparents, aunts and uncles, parents, children and grandchildren. In the 20th century, because of the emergence of the nuclear family, apartments have become the main form of housing, especially in urban areas.

In the cities in China, housing is traditionally provided by government employers, called dānwèi 单位. Workers lease their units from their dānwèi. The unit usually contains small rooms and the toilet is often shared by a few families. To save room, people often use the little veranda for cooking as well as for drying clothes. There are units containing better facilities for more affluent people, but they are not numerous. In the last twenty years, a private housing policy has been introduced, and people are being encouraged to buy their own units.

In the country, many families still have three generations living together, that is, grandparents, parents and children. After 1978, the commune system was dismantled, and agricultural production returned to being based on the family unit. A "free market" was established for farmers to earn extra money from selling surplus grain, fruit, vegetables and chickens. Some peasants have become wealthy and can afford to build their own houses or even two- or three-storey mansions equipped with better and more modern electrical facilities.

In Taiwan, the standard of living is similar to that of the West. Due to the high population density and the scarcity of land, people in the cities mainly live in high-rise buildings. However, there are still traditional U-shaped houses in country areas, although they are also disappearing, to be replaced with multi-storey buildings.

sìhéyuàn 四合院

dì sì kè   wǒ de yīfu
第四课 我的衣服

1 **What are they wearing?** 他们今天穿<ruby>穿<rt>chuān</rt></ruby>什么？

Huáng xiānsheng   xīzhuāng
黄先生穿西装；
tàitai   liányīqún
黄太太穿连衣裙。

Lín   chènshān   kùzi
林老师穿衬衫和裤子；
Lǐ   qípáo
李小姐穿旗袍。

Dàwěi   xùshān
大伟穿 T 恤衫；
mián'ǎo
小明穿棉袄。

兰兰穿毛衣、裙子
máoyī   qúnzi

wàitào
和外套。

2 How do they fit? 这些衣服怎么样？

这件衬衫太长了；

　　那件衬衫太短了。

这条裙子太肥了；

　　那条裙子太瘦了。

这条裤子太大了；

　　那条裤子太小了。

这件旗袍穿起来不舒服；

　　那条连衣裙看起来很漂亮。

3 **What clothes are there?**

bǎihuò shāngdiàn zhé mǎi
今天百货商店的衣服打七折。兰兰的妈妈买了

duō
很多衣服。她买了什么呢？

hóngsè qípáo
一件红色的旗袍
tiáo lǜsè liányīqún
一条绿色的连衣裙

báisè chènshān
一件白色的衬衫
hēisè máoyī
一件黑色的毛衣

lánsè mián'ǎo
一件蓝色的棉袄
wàitào
一件黄色的外套

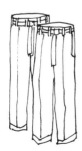
huīsè kùzi
两条灰色的裤子
zǐsè qúnzi
两条紫色的裙子

4 **What should I wear?**

 **Learn the sentences**

※ **Asking what someone is wearing**

To ask what clothes someone is wearing, use 穿什么衣服 chuān shénme yīfu. This is often shortened to 穿什么 chuān shénme. To answer, replace this phrase with a description of the clothes being worn.

他今天穿什么？ Lín 林老师昨天穿什么？	chènshān　　kùzi 他今天穿衬衫和裤子。 qípáo 她昨天穿旗袍。

※ **Describing how clothes fit**

When describing something using 太 tài- too, 了 le is usually used after the stative verb. For example, to say too big, say 太大了 tài dà le.

chènshān 这件衬衫怎么样？ máoyī 那件毛衣怎么样？ tiáo　　liányīqún 那条连衣裙怎么样？	duǎn 这件衬衫太短了。 那件毛衣太大了。 féi 那条连衣裙太肥了。

这件毛衣怎么样？

那件毛衣太短了。

✳ **Use of** 起来 qǐlai **after a verb**

The meaning of 起来 qǐlai is literally to stand up, to rise. However, it can be used after a verb to express an impression or an opinion of something.

这件棉袄 mián'ǎo 怎么样？	这件棉袄穿起来 qǐlai 很舒服 shūfu。
这件旗袍 qípáo 怎么样？	这件旗袍穿起来不舒服。
那条 tiáo 裤子 kùzi 怎么样？	那条裤子看起来很时髦 shímáo。

✳ **Stating a discount**

Stating a discount in Chinese is opposite to what is used in English. 10% off is said as 九折 jiǔ zhé; and 25% off is said as 七五折 qī wǔ zhé. To ask a discount, say 打几折 dǎ jǐ zhé.

这件衣服打几折 zhé？	这件衣服打七折。
这条 tiáo 裙子 qúnzi 打几折？	这条裙子打九折。
那条裤子 kùzi 打几折？	那条裤子打八五折。

✳ **Use of** 的 de **as a descriptive word**

We have learnt to use 的 de as a possessive word. It is used after a noun, often a person, to indicate the owner of something, i.e. 姐姐的书 jiějie de shū. The 的 de can also be used as a descriptive word. It is used after a noun or an adjective to describe the condition of something, i.e. 白色的衬衫 báisè de chènshān.

我有一件黄色的毛衣 máoyī。
姐姐喜欢穿紫色 zǐsè 的衣服。
黄老师今天穿了一条红色的连衣裙 liányīqún。

※ **Asking about someone's purchase**

To ask What clothes did you buy? say 你买了什么衣服？ Nǐ mǎi le shénme yīfu? To answer, replace 什么衣服 shénme yīfu with items being purchased.

你今天买了什么衣服？	我买了一条黑色的裤子。
姐姐今天买了什么衣服？	她买了三条红色的连衣裙。
爸爸昨天买了什么衣服？	他买了两件白色的衬衫。

※ **Asking what to wear**

Wondering what should be done, the word 该 gāi is used in front of a verb. To ask What should I wear? say, 我该穿什么？ Wǒ gāi chuān shénme? To answer, replace 什么 shénme with items being suggested.

我今天该穿什么？	穿 T 恤衫吧！
弟弟今天该穿什么？	他该穿衬衫和裤子。
哥哥今天该穿什么呢？	他今天该穿西装。

New words and expressions

衣服	yīfu	clothes, clothing yī- clothes; fú- clothes
穿	chuān	to wear (clothes, shoes or socks)
黄	Huáng	a family name huáng- yellow
先生	xiānsheng	Mr; (in Taiwan) husband xiān- first; shēng- to be born
西装	xīzhuāng	Western-style attire, suit xī- west; zhuāng- outfit
太太	tàitai	Mrs; (in Taiwan) wife tài- too, excessively
连衣裙	liányīqún	woman's dress, called 洋装 yángzhuāng in Taiwan lián- to join; yī- clothes; qún- skirt; yáng- foreign; zhuāng- outfit
衬衫	chènshān	shirt

裤子	kùzi	trousers, pants
小姐	xiǎojiě	Miss; young lady
旗袍	qípáo	a close-fitting dress with a high neck and a slit skirt
T恤衫	T xùshān	T-shirt
棉袄	mián'ǎo	cotton-padded coat　mián- cotton
毛衣	máoyī	sweater　máo- fur, feather; yī- clothes
裙子	qúnzi	skirt
外套	wàitào	coat　wài- outside; tào- cover
怎么样	zěnmeyàng	how about, what about
件	jiàn	[a measure word for clothing or affair]
太	tài	too, excessively
长	cháng	long
条	tiáo	[a measure word for trousers, shorts, skirt etc]
肥	féi	loose-fitting (clothing), (宽 kuān is used in Taiwan); fat
瘦	shòu	tight-fitting (clothing), (窄 zhǎi is used in Taiwan); thin
起来	qǐlai	[indicating impressions]
舒服	shūfu	comfortable　shū- comfortable
漂亮	piàoliang	pretty　piào- pretty; liàng- bright, shining
百货商店	bǎihuò shāngdiàn	department store　bǎi- hundred; huò- goods; shāng- business; diàn- shop
打折	dǎzhé	discount　zhé- fold
买	mǎi	to buy
多	duō	much, many
红色	hóngsè	red　hóng- red; sè- colour
绿色	lǜsè	green　lǜ- green
白色	báisè	white　bái- white, Bái- a surname
黑色	hēisè	black　hēi- black
蓝色	lánsè	blue　lán- blue
黄色	huángsè	yellow　huáng- yellow, Huáng- a surname
灰色	huīsè	grey　huī- grey
紫色	zǐsè	purple　zǐ- purple
该	gāi	should
好看	hǎokàn	good-looking
时髦	shímáo	fashion, fashionable
挺	tǐng	[oral] very
唉	ài	(a sigh)

Write the characters

衣 yī *clothes*	服 fú *clothes*	穿 chuān *to wear*	黄 huáng; Huáng *yellow; a surname*	先 xiān *first*
太 tài *too, excessively*	怎 zěn *how*	样 yàng *appearance*	件 jiàn *[measure word]*	红 hóng *red*
色 sè *colour*	绿 lǜ *green*	白 bái; Bái *white; a surname*	黑 hēi *black*	蓝 lán *blue*

太 时髦 了
shímáo

王利的妹妹有很多衣服：衬衫、
　　　　　　　　　　　　　chènshān

裙子、毛衣、外套、连衣裙；白色的，
qúnzi　máoyī　wàitào　liányīqún

黑色的，红色的，黄色的，蓝色的，绿

色的,很多很多。今天她不知道该穿什么，
　　　　duō　　　　　　zhīdào　gāi

她说："这件太大了，那件太小了；这件

太长了，那件太短了；这条太肥了，那
cháng　　　　duǎn　　　tiáo　féi

条太瘦了。我今天穿
shòu

什么呢？唉！我今天
　　ài

没有衣服穿！"

Something to know

❀ Traditional clothes today

Some clothing worn by the Chinese today still retains the Mandarin style of the Qing dynasty, but with some modifications. Qípáo 旗袍 and mián'ǎo 棉袄 are the two most popular styles. Qípáo is a close-fitting dress with a high neck and a slit skirt. It is still regarded as women's formal dress. Mián'ǎo is a cotton-padded jacket. The softness and warmth of the jacket makes it ideal for the cold winter. Chángpáo mǎguà 长袍马褂, a mandarin jacket worn over a gown by men, is no longer everyday wear but is worn on the stage, particularly by those who perform xiàngshēng 相声, a comic dialogue. The best material for this clothing is silk.

A style, in white, worn by Dr Sun Yat-sen called Zhōngshānzhuāng 中山装, was once popular, and the style, in blue, worn by Nikolai Lenin called Lièníngzhuāng 列宁装 became popular in China after China became a communist country in 1949. However, both styles have now become unfashionable.

❀ Chinese silk

Silk cloth in China dates back to the Neolithic period, around 7000 to 1600 BC. Silk is produced from the cocoons of silkworms, which are raised on woven trays and fed with hand-picked mulberry leaves. Before the moths emerge, the cocoons are plunged into boiling

People wearing the traditional clothing chángpáo mǎguà 长袍马褂
acting the comic dialogue xiàngshēng 相声

water and the silk fibre is reeled off. With care, the fibre can be reeled off in a continuous unbroken thread to an average length of around 500 metres. The silk fibre is then used to produce a luxurious textile. Silk is light, soft, smooth and durable.

In the early days, silk was the favourite textile of the imperial family and was often used as gifts for rulers of other countries. The Silk Road, a route from China to overseas, was gradually formed due to the export of silk to Japan and to the West. Today, silk is still one of the main exports of China. The embroidery of Sūzhōu 苏州, called sūxiù 苏绣, and that of Húnán 湖南, called xiāngxiù 湘绣, are world famous.

❀ Chinese colours

Traditionally, Chinese regarded white as the colour of mourning and red as the colour of luck. Before the influence of the West and the popularity of the white wedding dress in the 20th century, Chinese brides wore red wedding dresses. Yellow is particularly associated with the emperor. The garment of the emperor was described as the Yellow Robe, Huángpáo 黄袍, which is normally decorated with dragons. Gold, the colour of wealth, green,

the colour of prosperity, and red were used for the decorations of the imperial palace and are still widely used in many Taoist temples in Taiwan.

About Pinyin and characters

Sound separation in Pinyin

Pinyin of characters in a word are usually written together. When the second character starts with a vowel, i.e. a, o or e, an apostrophe is placed before the vowel to separate the sound between two characters so as to avoid confusion.

棉袄	mián'ǎo, Chinese winter garment		可爱	kě'ài, lovely
木偶	mù'ǒu, puppet		配偶	pèi'ǒu, spouse
十二	shí'èr, twelve		星期二	xīngqī'èr, Tuesday

dì wǔ kè   fùxí   yī
第五课 复习（一）

1 A profile

黄蓝明是一九七八

年生的。他的眉毛(méimao)很长(cháng)，

眼睛(yǎnjing)和鼻子(bízi)都小，嘴巴(zuǐba)不

小。他家是楼房(lóufáng)，家里有爸爸、妈妈和一个弟弟。

今天是五月二十四日，星期六，也是黄蓝明的生日。

黄蓝明今天七点十分起床(qǐchuáng)，七点半吃早饭，八点在房间听(tīng)

音乐(yīnyuè)。九点五十分，他在浴室(yùshì)里，不知道(zhīdào)在做什么；十点

二十五分，他在车库(chēkù)里，也不知道在做什么。

黄蓝明今天上午穿绿色的 T 恤衫(xùshān)和黑色的裤子(kùzi)，下午

穿白色的衬衫(chènshān)和蓝色的裤子。现在是下午三点四十六分。

黄蓝明的爸爸和妈妈在客厅(kètīng)喝茶(chá)，弟弟在厨房(chúfáng)吃黄蓝明的

生日蛋糕(dàngāo)。黄蓝明在厕所(cèsuǒ)里，不知道在做什么。

2 Language functions

[1] Asking the date

今天是几月几号？ Jīntiān shì jǐ yuè jǐ hào?

今天是五月二十九号。 Jīntiān shì wǔ yuè èrshíjiǔ hào.

Asking the day of the week

昨天是星期几？ Zuótiān shì xīngqī jǐ?

昨天是星期四。 Zuótiān shì xīngqīsì.

Stating the date

今天是二〇〇八年六月十三日，星期四。

Jīntiān shì èr líng líng bā nián liù yuè shísān rì, xīngqīsì.

后天是二〇〇八年六月十五日，星期六。

Hòutiān shì èr líng líng bā nián liù yuè shíwǔ rì, xīngqīliù.

Asking whose birthday it is

前天是谁的生日？ Qiántiān shì shéi de shēngrì?

前天是我哥哥的生日。 Qiántiān shì wǒ gēge de shēngrì.

Asking about birthdays

你的生日是什么时候？ Nǐ de shēngrì shì shénme shíhou?

我的生日是七月十四日。 Wǒ de shēngrì shì qī yuè shísì rì.

Asking the year someone was born

你是哪年生的？ Nǐ shì nǎ nián shēng de?

我是一九九六年生的。 Wǒ shì yī jiǔ jiǔ liù nián shēng de.

[2] Asking what someone is doing

你在做什么？ Nǐ zài zuò shénme?

我在做功课。 Wǒ zài zuò gōngkè.

Asking the time

现在几点？ Xiànzài jǐ diǎn?

现在四点半。 Xiànzài sì diǎn bàn.

现在几点了？ Xiànzài jǐ diǎn le?

现在四点五十五分了。 Xiànzài sì diǎn wǔshíwǔ fēn le.

Asking what time someone does something

你几点上学？ Nǐ jǐ diǎn shàngxué?

我八点半上学。 Wǒ bā diǎn bàn shàngxué.

你晚上几点睡觉？ Nǐ wǎnshang jǐ diǎn shuìjiào?

我晚上十点睡觉。 Wǒ wǎnshang shí diǎn shuìjiào.

Use of "了 le"

太好了。 Tài hǎo le.

我知道了。 Wǒ zhīdào le.

现在几点了。 Xiànzài jǐ diǎn le.

好了！好了！ Hǎo le! Hǎo le!

弟弟上学了。 Dìdi shàngxué le.

[3] Stating relative locations

我在左边；你在右边。 Wǒ zài zuǒbian; nǐ zài yòubian.

爸爸在前面；妈妈在后面。 Bàba zài qiánmian; māma zài hòumian.

Asking the location of something/someone

哥哥在哪儿？ Gēge zài nǎr?

哥哥在他的房间。 Gēge zài tā de fángjiān.

我的手机呢？ Wǒ de shǒujī ne?

你的手机在电脑上面。 Nǐ de shǒujī zài diànnǎo shàngmian.

Asking what someone is doing somewhere

弟弟在客厅做什么？ Dìdi zài kètīng zuò shénme?

他在客厅看电视。 Tā zài kètīng kàn diànshì.

Use of "呢 ne" in a question

我喜欢打乒乓球，你呢？ Wǒ xǐhuān dǎ pīngpāngqiú, nǐ ne?

我的书呢？ Wǒ de shū ne?

你的狗在哪儿呢？ Nǐ de gǒu zài nǎr ne?

[4] Asking what someone is wearing

姐姐今天穿什么？ Jiějie jīntiān chuān shénme?

她今天穿连衣裙。 Tā jīntiān chuān liányīqún.

Describing how clothes fit

这件外套怎么样？ Zhè jiàn wàitào zěnmeyàng?

这件外套太大了。 Zhè jiàn wàitào tài dà le.

那条裤子怎么样？ Nà tiáo kùzi zěnmeyàng?

那条裤子太肥了。 Nà tiáo kùzi tài féi le.

Use of "起来 qǐlai" after a verb

那条裙子穿起来不舒服。 Nà tiáo qúnzi chuān qǐlai bù shūfu.

这件毛衣看起来很时髦。 Zhè jiàn máoyī kàn qǐlai hěn shímáo.

Stating a discount

今天的衣服打几折？ Jīntiān de yīfu dǎ jǐ zhé?

今天的衣服都打八折。 Jīntiān de yīfu dōu dǎ bā zhé.

那条裤子打几折？ Nà tiáo kùzi dǎ jǐ zhé?

那条裤子打七五折。 Nà tiáo kùzi dǎ qī wǔ zhé.

Use of "的 de" as a descriptive word

妹妹穿了一条红色的裙子。 Mèimei chuān le yì tiáo hóngsè de qúnzi.

哥哥有五件蓝色的衬衫。 Gēge yǒu wǔ jiàn lánsè de chènshān.

Asking about someone's purchase

你今天买了什么衣服？ Nǐ jīntiān mǎi le shénme yīfu?

我买了一条裤子。 Wǒ mǎi le yì tiáo kùzi.

姐姐今天买了什么衣服？ Jiějie jīntiān mǎi le shénme yīfu?

她买了三件紫色的连衣裙。 Tā mǎi le sān jiàn zǐsè de liányīqún.

Asking what to wear

姐姐今天该穿什么？ Jiějie jīntiān gāi chuān shénme?

她今天该穿旗袍。 Tā jīntiān gāi chuān qípáo.

dì liù kè mǎi dōngxi

第六课 买东西

1 **At the shop**

shāngdiàn mǎi dōngxi

今天兰兰去商店买东西。

běn duōshǎo qián

这本书多少钱？

kuài

十八块。

xiàngpí

这个橡皮多少钱？

三块。

bǐ

这笔多少钱？

三块半。

jiǎndāo

这剪刀多少钱？

九块半。

zìdiǎn

这字典多少钱？

máo

二十块六毛。

dìtú

这地图多少钱？

九块九毛五。

yígòng

一共多少钱？

一共六十四块五毛五。

2 **At the market** 今天小明去市场买水果。
shìchǎng　shuǐguǒ

3 At the clothes shop 今天大伟去服装店买裤子。
Dàwěi　fúzhuāng diàn　kùzi

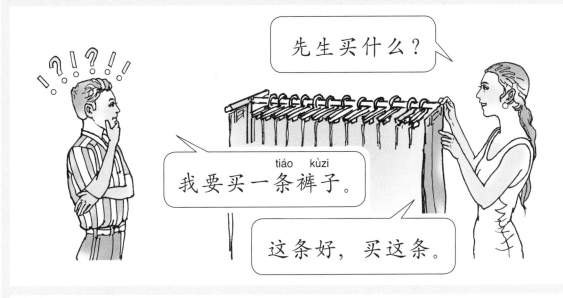

先生买什么？

我要买一条裤子。
tiáo　kùzi

这条好，买这条。

那条多少钱？

一百五十八块。

太贵了，有没有便宜一点儿的？
guì
piányi　yìdiǎnr

这条便宜一点儿，九十七块。

还是贵，有没有更便宜的？
háishi　gèng

这条更便宜，三十六块。

 **Learn the sentences**

✳ **Asking the price**

To state an amount of money, use 块 kuài for dollars and 毛 máo for ten-cent units. 分 fēn, which is used for cents from one to nine, is now rarely used. The last unit word can be omitted when making the statement. When the amount ends in 50 cents, 半 bàn or 五 is often used instead. To ask How much is this book? say 这本书多少钱？ Zhè běn shū duōshǎo qián? In spoken Chinese, a measure word that follows 这 can also be omitted.

¥1.00: 一块 / 元 yuán	¥0.10: 一毛 / 角 jiǎo	¥0.01: 一分
¥0.50: 五毛 / 角 jiǎo	¥1.50: 一块半 or 一块五	

这本书多少钱？ běn	二十块。
这字典多少钱？ zìdiǎn	二十块半。
这衣服多少钱？	二十块八毛。
这裤子多少钱？ kùzi	二十块八毛五。

这条裤子多少钱？

一百六十块。

✳ **Asking how things are sold**

To ask *How are the apples sold?* say 苹果怎么卖？Píngguǒ zěnme mài? The reply will depend on the selling unit, e.g. by weight, say 一斤 yì jīn, or by item, say 一个 yí gè, then followed by the price.

píngguǒ 苹果怎么卖？	jīn 苹果一斤三块。
xiāngjiāo 香蕉怎么卖？	香蕉一斤三块半。
xīguā 西瓜怎么卖？	一个八块九毛五。

One can also ask the price by weight or item. To ask, use 一斤 yì jīn or 一个 yí gè followed by 多少钱 duōshǎo qián.

píngguǒ　　jīn 苹果一斤多少钱？	苹果一斤五块半。
cǎoméi 草莓一斤多少钱？	草莓一斤九块五。
bōluó 菠萝一个多少钱？	菠萝一个三块四毛九。

✳ **Expressing the degree of an opinion**

To express an opinion, there are various degrees of description that can be used. For extremely expensive, say 非常贵 fēicháng guì; for very expensive, say 很贵 hěn guì; for not expensive, say 不贵 bú guì and for not expensive at all, say 一点儿都不贵 yìdiǎnr dōu bú guì.

fēicháng 非常贵	很贵	不贵	dōu 一点儿都不贵
非常便宜	很便宜	不便宜	一点儿都不便宜
tián 非常甜	很甜	不甜	一点儿都不甜
suān 非常酸	很酸	不酸	一点儿都不酸

lóngyǎn
龙眼贵吗？

fēicháng
龙眼非常贵。

píngguǒ
苹果便宜吗？

苹果很便宜。

xīguā
西瓜便宜吗？

西瓜不便宜。

júzi suān
橘子酸不酸？

橘子一点儿都不酸。

✳ Making comparisons

To compare the degree of something, 一点儿 yìdiǎnr and 更 gèng can be used. For slightly more expensive, say 贵一点儿 guì yìdiǎnr; for even more expensive, say 更贵 gèng guì.

这个便宜	那个贵一点儿	那个更贵
这个贵	那个便宜一点儿	那个更便宜
这件大	那件小一点儿	那件更小

Sour grapes

你今天买了什么？

lizhī   jīn
我买了荔枝，一斤十块。

tián
甜吗？

很甜。

你还买了什么？

júzi
我还买了橘子，一斤四块半。

甜不甜？

fēicháng
非常甜。

你还买了什么？

bōluó
我还买了菠萝，一个三块六。

suān
酸不酸？

一点儿都不酸。
你想吃什么？荔枝、
橘子还是菠萝？

tián   suān pútáo
我今天不想吃甜的；我想吃酸葡萄。

✳ **Asking for another option**

To ask for a choice, express an opinion then ask for an alternative, either by price, by size, by colour or by others.

这个太贵了，有没有便宜一点儿的？

这件太小了，有没有大一点儿的？

这条太长了，有没有短一点儿的？
_{tiáo　cháng　　　　duǎn}

这个还是贵，有没有更便宜的？

这件还是小，有没有更大的？

这条还是长，有没有更短的？
_{tiáo　cháng　　　　duǎn}

我不要白色的，有没有黑色的？

我不要红色的，有没有绿色的？

 New words and expressions

商店	shāngdiàn	shop shāng- business; diàn- shop
本	běn	[a measure word for books, magazines etc]
多少	duōshǎo	how much, how many duō- many, much; shǎo- few, little
钱	qián	money
块	kuài	[oral] monetary unit for dollar, formally called 元 yuán
字典	zìdiǎn	dictionary zì- word, character
毛	máo	1. [oral] 10-cent unit, formally called 角 jiǎo; 2. fur
地图	dìtú	map dì- ground; tú- picture

一共	yígòng	all together yī- one; gòng- together
市场	shìchǎng	market shì- market, city; chǎng- field
水果	shuǐguǒ	fruit shuǐ- water; guǒ- fruit
香蕉	xiāngjiāo	banana xiāng- fragrant; jiāo- a broadleaf plant
怎么	zěnme	how, what
卖	mài	to sell
斤	jīn	a unit of weight (= 0.5 kilograms) (kilogram- 公斤 gōngjīn)
草莓	cǎoméi	strawberry cǎo- straw; méi- berry
龙眼	lóngyǎn	longan lóng- dragon; yǎn- eye
荔枝	lìzhī	lychee
菠萝	bōluó	pineapple, also called 凤梨 fènglí
西瓜	xīguā	watermelon xī- west; guā- melon
葡萄	pútáo	grapes
甜	tián	sweet
非常	fēicháng	extremely fēi- not; cháng- usually, often
橘子	júzi	mandarin, tangerine
酸	suān	sour
苹果	píngguǒ	apple
要	yào	to want, would like
服装店	fúzhuāngdiàn	clothes shop
贵	guì	expensive, dear
便宜	piányi	cheap, inexpensive
一点儿	yìdiǎnr	a little (can be shortened as 点儿) diǎn- dot, o'clock; (é)r- [a word ending]
还是	háishi	still
更	gèng	even, even more
中号	zhōng hào	medium size
小号	xiǎo hào	small size (large size- 大号 dà hào)
给	gěi	to give
找	zhǎo	to give change
您	nín	[polite form] you
元	yuán	[formal] monetary unit for dollar
分	fēn	one-cent unit

Write the characters

买 mǎi — *to buy*	多 duō — *many, much*	少 shǎo — *few, little*	钱 qián — *money*	块 kuài — *dollar*
毛 máo — *10-cent unit; fur*	共 gòng — *together*	卖 mài — *to sell*	要 yào — *to want, would like*	贵 guì — *expensive, dear*
便 pián — *cheap*	宜 yí — *suitable*	还 hái — *also, still*	更 gèng — *even, even more*	给 gěi — *to give*

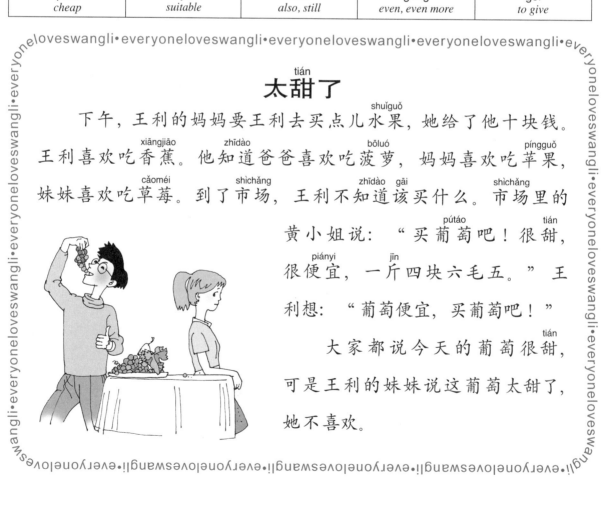

太甜了
tián

　　下午，王利的妈妈要王利去买点儿水果，她给了他十块钱。
王利喜欢吃香蕉。他知道爸爸喜欢吃菠萝，妈妈喜欢吃苹果，
妹妹喜欢吃草莓。到了市场，王利不知道该买什么。市场里的

黄小姐说："买葡萄吧！很甜，很便宜，一斤四块六毛五。"王
利想："葡萄便宜，买葡萄吧！"

大家都说今天的葡萄很甜，可是王利的妹妹说这葡萄太甜了，
她不喜欢。

Something to know

❀ The currencies in China and Taiwan

The currency used in China is called rénmínbì 人民币, people's money, and the monetary symbol is ¥. The currency used in Taiwan is called xīntáibì 新台币, new currency of Taiwan, and the monetary symbol is $. The numbers used on notes and coins are in a complicated form, i.e. 壹（一）、贰（二）、叁（三）、肆（四）、伍（五）、陆（六）、柒（七）、捌（八）、玖（九）、拾（十）. Cheques are also written in this form so they cannot be easily altered. Commodity prices in China, although varying at times, are generally much lower than in Australia or in America.

Notes and coins used in China　　　　*Notes and coins used in Taiwan*

❀ Shopping and bargaining

Chinese people like fresh food. Most people buy what they need in the local market every day. Local markets are busy and lively. They are stocked with fruit, fish, meat, live chickens, freshly picked vegetable and groceries. Bargaining is commonly practised here. In town, there are shops and big department stores. Prices in these stores are generally fixed, although some may still have a little room for bargaining.

A scene in a free market

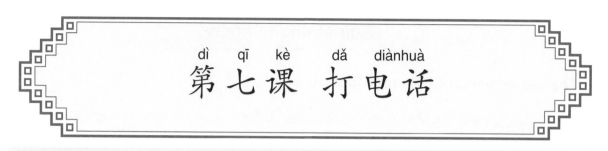

dì qī kè dǎ diànhuà
第七课 打电话

1 Not home

wèi　　qǐngwèn Lánlan
喂！请问兰兰在家吗？

nín　　　wèi
兰兰不在家。您是哪位？

Dàwěi
我是兰兰的同学，白大伟。

shì chūqù
兰兰有事出去了。

shíhou huílái
请问她什么时候回来？

她下午两点左右回来。

zài　　　　zàijiàn
那我下午再打来。再见。

再见。

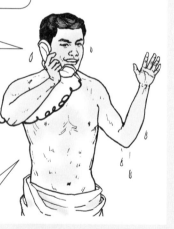

2 **What's your telephone number?**

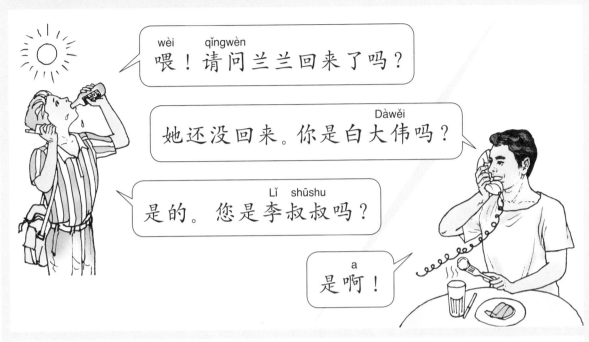

喂！请问兰兰回来了吗？

她还没回来。你是白大伟吗？

是的。您是李叔叔吗？

是啊！

李叔叔好！兰兰回来时，请她打电话给我，好吗？

好啊！你的电话号码是多少？

我的电话号码是九八七六五四三二。
我的手机号码是〇一二三九八七六五四。

3 Wait a moment, please

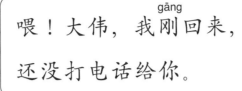

喂！大伟，我刚(gāng)回来，还没打电话给你。

没关系(guānxì)。你明天有空(kòng)吗？

我上午没空，下午有空。有什么事吗？

明天是我的生日。我们明天晚上要去中国城(Zhōngguóchéng)吃饭。我想请你一块儿(yíkuàir)去。

那太好了，谢谢你。明天几点？

下午六点半左右。我们来接(jiē)你，可以(kěyǐ)吗？

行(xíng)，明天见(jiàn)。

Learn the sentences

✳ **Asking if someone is home**

To ask if someone is home, use 在家吗 zài jiā ma. To reply yes to the question, say 在 zài; to reply no, say 不在 bú zài.

qǐngwèn Wáng 请问 王 先生在家吗？	他在。
请问黄小姐在家吗？	她不在。
你爸爸在家吗？	他不在家。您是哪位？

✳ **Asking when someone is coming back**

To ask When are you coming back? say 你什么时候回来？ Nǐ shénme shíhou huílái?, or 你几点回来？ Nǐ jǐ diǎn huílái? if only clock time is expected for the answer.

你什么时候回来？	明天上午九点。
你爸爸什么时候回来？	他九月二十五号回来。
你妈妈几点回来？	她下午两点半回来。

✳ **Asking who is speaking on the telephone**

To ask Who is speaking? say 您是哪位？ Nín shì nǎ/něi wèi? To answer, say your name or
your relationship to the person being sought.

您是哪位？ ^{wèi}	我是兰兰的同学。
您是哪位？	我是李叔叔。 ^{Lǐ shūshu}
请问您是哪位？	我是王老师。 ^{Wáng}

✳ **Asking if someone has come back**

To ask Has he come back? say 他回来了吗？ Tā huílái le ma? To answer yes, say 他回来了。
Tā huílái le. To answer no, say 他还没回来。 Tā hái méi huílái. Notice the use of 了 le for a
completed action as learnt in Lesson 2.

请问，林老师回来了吗？ ^{Lín}	他回来了。
爸爸回来了吗？	他还没回来。
你哥哥回来了吗？	回来了。
你妹妹回来了吗？	还没。

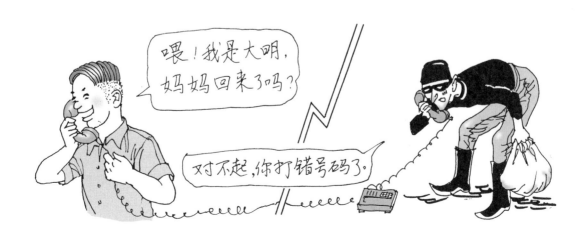

✳ **Asking someone's telephone number**

To ask someone's telephone number, use the question word 多少 duōshǎo. To answer the question, replace 多少 duōshǎo with the number. In a telephone number, 一 is often pronounced as yāo.

你家的电话号码是多少？ *hàomǎ*	我家的电话号码是六四〇五五三三。
你的手机号码是多少？ *shǒujī*	我的手机号码是〇二三七八五六六五。
他的电话号码是多少？	他的电话号码是五六九六四六四。
你哥哥的电话号码是多少？	他的电话号码是八九〇一二三四。 *yāo*

✳ **Asking someone who he/she is looking for**

To ask Who are you looking for? say 你找谁？ Nǐ zhǎo shéi? or more politely say 您找哪位？ Nín zhǎo nǎ/něi wèi? To answer, replace 谁 shéi or 哪位 nǎ/něi wèi with the person's name or title.

你找谁？	我找白先生。
您找哪位？ *wèi*	我找你爸爸。
您找哪位？	我找林老师。 *Lín*

❋ **Asking if someone is available**

To ask if someone is available, use either 有空吗 yǒu kòng ma or 有没有空 yǒu méi yǒu kòng. To answer yes, say 有 yǒu; to answer no, say 没有 méi yǒu. 没有 méi yǒu is often shortened as 没 méi in a statement, e.g. 我没空 Wǒ méi kòng.

你明天有空吗？	我明天没空。
你今天下午有空吗？	我下午有空。
你后天有没有空？	我后天没空。
你九月十三日有空吗？	有啊！有什么事吗？

❋ **Seeking agreement**

To ask for an agreement, state the activity followed by 可以吗？ kěyǐ ma? To answer yes, say 可以 kěyǐ or 行 xíng. To answer no, say 不行 bù xíng.

我明天来接你，可以吗？	行，明天见。
我明天去看你，可以吗？	不行，我明天有事。
我明天请你吃饭，可以吗？	行，你请我吃什么？
你明天请我吃饭，可以吗？	不行，我明天没空。

A blind date

About Pinyin and characters

Use of 儿 er at word end

When 儿 is used as a word end, it only adds a tongue-curling sound r to the preceding character. The ending of the preceding character is often dropped when spoken, e.g. 一点儿 is written as yìdiǎnr in Pinyin but pronounced as yìdiǎr.

Phrase	Pinyin	Pronounced
一点儿，a bit, a little	yìdiǎnr	(yìdiǎr)
一块儿，together	yíkuàir	(yíkuàr)
一会儿，a little while	yíhuìr	(yíhùr)

New words and expressions

在家	zàijiā	at home
哪位	nǎ/něi wèi	which one (person)　哪 is often pronounced as něi when directly followed by a measure word
事	shì	matter, thing, business
出去	chūqù	to go out　chū- out; qù- to go
回来	huílái	to come back, to return　huí- to return; lái- to come
左右	zuǒyòu	around, approximately　zuǒ- left; yòu- right
那	nà	then, in that case, short for 那么 nàme
再	zài	again
叔叔	shūshu	father's younger brother; also used to address men of father's age
… … 时	… shí	when...　shí- time
号码	hàomǎ	number
找	zhǎo	1. to look for; 2. to give change
等	děng	to wait
一会儿	yíhuìr	a little while
马上	mǎshàng	right away　mǎ- horse; shàng- up, above
刚	gāng	just
空	kòng	free time, spare time
中国城	Zhōngguóchéng	Chinatown　Zhōngguó- China; chéng- town
一块儿	yíkuàir	together　kuài- lump, dollar
接	jiē	1. to meet, to pick (someone) up; 2. to answer the telephone
可以	kěyǐ	can, may　kě- may, be permitted; yǐ- so as to
行	xíng	all right, OK
咖啡色	kāfēisè	brown　kāfēi- coffee

Write the characters

电 diàn *electricity*	话 huà *speech*	请 qǐng *please; to invite*	您 nín *you [polite form]*	事 shì *matter, thing, business*
时 shí *time, hour*	候 hòu *time*	回 huí *to return*	来 lái *to come*	再 zài *again*
找 zhǎo *to look for; to give change*	等 děng *to wait*	空 kòng *free time, spare time*	可 kě *may, be permitted*	以 yǐ *so as to*

everyoneloveswangli•everyoneloveswangli•everyoneloveswangli•everyoneloveswangli•every

太晚了

　　今天王利有空，他想找林朋到他家玩儿。上午十点半，他打电话给林朋，接电话的是林朋的爸爸。他说林朋去中国城（Zhōngguóchéng）买东西（dōngxi），下午一点半左右回来。下午两点，王利再打电话，接电话的是林朋的姐姐。她说林朋去买字典（zìdiǎn），马上回来。三点二十分，王利再打电话，接电话的是林朋的妹妹。她说林朋在厕所（cèsuǒ），请他等一会儿（yìhuìr）。三点四十分，林朋接了电话，他说："对不起（duìbuqǐ），太晚了，我不去你家了，你来我家吧！"

Something to know

❀ Chinatown and Chinese migrants

Historically Chinese migrants are dispersed around the world. There are Chinatowns in the cities of the United States, Canada, Japan and Australia etc. Chinatowns, Zhōngguóchéng 中国城, are also called Tángrénjiē 唐人街, namely Chinese street. Typical shops in Chinatowns are Chinese grocery stores, medicine shops, restaurants and gift shops.

Chinese migration dates back to 540 AD, with around 7,000 families residing in Japan at that time. Most migrants left China after the 16th century, when Chinese labourers were transported by some Western countries to their colonies as coolies. Some people on the southeast coast of China, where the land is poor, moved to southeast Asia to seek a better living and gradually settled there. During the gold rush in the United States and in Australia, Chinese gold diggers went and sought their fortunes. Many of them settled in the United States. In Australia, the number of Chinese immigrants decreased dramatically after the introduction of the White Australia Policy, but still a small number settled down. Many Chinese started businesses such as laundries and restaurants. A Chinese dialect, Cantonese Guǎngdōnghuà 广东话, was commonly spoken by these migrants.

The recent wave of Chinese migrants in the 20th century are people from many different social backgrounds. They are postgraduate students, businessmen and skilled persons from Taiwan and Hong Kong, as well as from China. As these recent migrants speak Mandarin, Mandarin has become popular in the local community and in Chinatown. However, except for those from China who use simplified characters, most Chinese migrants still read and write traditional characters. Local Chinese newspapers and publications are mostly printed in the traditional form. Many weekend Chinese schools are also teaching Chinese in the traditional form.

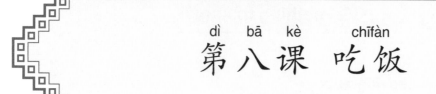

dì bā kè chīfàn
第八课　吃饭

1 At the restaurant

Lánlan　　　Dàwěi　　　　　　　Zhōngguóchéng
今天兰兰和大伟一家人去中国城吃饭。

huānyíng guānglín　　　　　cài dān
欢迎光临！这是菜单。

xièxie
谢谢。今天我来点菜。

您点什么菜？

什么菜好吃？

gǔlǎoròu　　　mápó dòufu dōu
古老肉和麻婆豆腐都不错。

pán
好！来一盘古老肉，一盘

shīzitóu
麻婆豆腐，一盘狮子头和

chǎo qīngcài
一盘炒青菜。

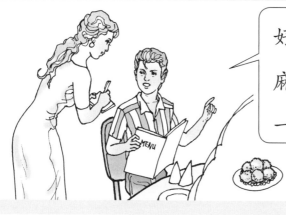

2 Always Chinese food

大伟，昨天的菜真好吃。谢谢你！

不客气。那家饭馆的菜做得不错。
kèqi fànguǎn de

你们常去中国饭馆吃饭吗？
cháng

我们常去。因为我爸爸喜欢
吃中国菜，所以我们常常去。
你们呢？常去饭馆吃饭吗？
yīnwèi suǒyǐ

我们不常去饭馆吃饭。因为我妈妈
菜做得很好，所以我们不常去。

你们平常都吃中国菜吗？
píngcháng

我们平常都吃中国菜。下个星期六
到我们家吃饭吧！

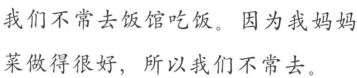

3 **Being a guest**　今天兰兰请大伟去她家吃饭。

> 这是我同学，白大伟。

> huānyíng
> 欢迎你来，大伟。

> 这是我爸爸、妈妈。

> shūshu　āyí
> 叔叔、阿姨好。

> 好，好！请坐，大伟！ zuò

> 谢谢！

> chá
> 来，请喝茶。

> 谢谢！

Learn the sentences

✳ Ordering food

To ask guests to order food from a menu, say 您点什么菜？ Nín diǎn shénme cài? To order, one can say 我们要 ... Wǒmen yào... or simply 来 ... Lái....

您点什么菜？	来一盘古老肉和一盘青菜。 <small>pán gǔlǎoròu qīngcài</small>
先生，点什么菜？	来一盘麻婆豆腐和一盘青菜。 <small>mápó dòufu</small>
小姐，点什么菜？	来一盘狮子头和一碗酸辣汤。 <small>shīzitóu wǎn suānlàtāng</small>

✳ Offering a choice

When offering a choice, use 还是 háishi which means or. To ask Would you like to eat plain rice or fried rice? say 你要吃米饭还是炒饭？ Nǐ yào chī mǐfàn háishi chǎofàn?

您要吃米饭还是炒饭？	吃炒饭。
您要喝茶还是喝果汁？ <small>guǒzhī</small>	喝果汁。
你要买衬衫还是 T 恤衫？ <small>chènshān xùshān</small>	我要买衬衫。
你要红色的还是白色的？	我要白色的。
你要去打篮球还是去游泳？ <small>lánqiú yóuyǒng</small>	我要去打篮球。
你喜欢游泳还是打球？	我喜欢打球。
那条裙子太肥还是太瘦？ <small>tiáo qúnzi féi shòu</small>	那条裙子太瘦了。

✳ **Expressing usually or often**

To say that someone does something often, use 常常 chángcháng or 常 cháng, and to say not often, use 不常 bù cháng. To say that someone usually does something, use 平常 píngcháng.

常常；常 often	我们常常去饭馆吃饭。 我星期天常去游泳。
不常 not often	我不常去中国饭馆吃饭。 我不常去百货商店。
平常 usually (often followed by 都)	我们平常都吃中国菜。 我平常都很早起床。

✳ **Explaining cause**

To state a cause and its consequence, use 因为 yīnwèi...... 所以 suǒyǐ...... or just use 所以 suǒyǐ...... alone.

因为中国菜好吃，所以我妈妈常做中国菜。 因为今天的菜好吃，所以我吃得太多了。 因为这西瓜很便宜，所以我买了两个。 因为那件衣服太贵了，所以我不买。 那葡萄太酸了，所以他不吃。

✳ **Expressions used by the host**

When visiting a Chinese family, one can often hear the polite expressions used by the host.

Upon arrival	
欢迎你来。 huānyíng	谢谢。
请进，请进！ jìn	谢谢。
请坐，请坐！ zuò	谢谢。
来，请喝茶。	谢谢。
At the dining table	
来，你坐这儿。 zuò	好，谢谢。
你自己来。 zìjǐ	好，我自己来。
别客气。 bié	我不客气。
今天没什么菜。	您太客气了。
多吃点儿。	我吃很多了，谢谢。

New words and expressions

光临	guānglín	[polite form] gracious presence (of guests)
菜单	càidān	menu cài- dish, vegetable; dān- list
点菜	diǎncài	to order dishes from a menu diǎn- to point, o'clock, dot; cài- dish, vegetable
古老肉	gǔlǎoròu	sweet and sour pork gǔ- ancient; lǎo- old; ròu- meat
麻婆豆腐	mápó-dòufu	name of a hot and spicy bean curd dish dòufu- bean curd
不错	búcuò	pretty good, not bad
来……	lái...	to give (us/me) ... (used when ordering food) lái- to come
盘	pán	[a measure word for dish] plate
狮子头	shīzitóu	name of a dish of fried meatballs shīzi- lion; tóu- head
炒	chǎo	to stir-fry
青菜	qīngcài	green vegetable
汤	tāng	soup

碗	wǎn	[a measure word for rice or soup] bowl
酸辣汤	suānlàtāng	hot and sour soup suān- sour; là- hot (spicy)
对了	duìle	by the way duì- correct, right
放	fàng	1. to put; 2. to let go
味精	wèijīng	monosodium glutamate (MSG)
没问题	méi wèntí	no problems wèn- to ask; tí- topic
米饭	mǐfàn	plain rice, called 白饭 báifàn in Taiwan
		mǐ- uncooked rice
还是	háishi	1. or; 2. still
汽水	qìshuǐ	soft drink, soda pop qì- steam, vapour
客气	kèqi	courteous kè- guest; qì- air
饭馆	fànguǎn	restaurant, or said 餐馆 cānguǎn guǎn- building
常	cháng	often, also said 常常 chángcháng
上	shàng	1. to go to; 2. up, above
因为	yīnwèi	because yīn- cause; wèi- for
所以	suǒyǐ	therefore suǒ- so; place; yǐ- so as to
平常	píngcháng	usually píng- flat; cháng- often
阿姨	āyí	used to address women of mother's age;
		(in southern regions) mother's sister yí- mother's sister
坐	zuò	to sit (sit down please- 请坐 qǐng zuò)
自己	zìjǐ	self (to help oneself- 自己来 zìjǐ lái)
别	bié	don't, do not
进	jìn	to enter (come in please- 请进 qǐng jìn)
旁边	pángbiān	side

About Pinyin and characters

Early Writing

坐 to sit, was earlier written as 坐 , which represents two people sitting face to face on the floor;

米 rice, was earlier written as 米 or 米 , which are pictures of rice grains on the plant;

肉 meat, was earlier written as 肉 , which is a picture of the body muscle;

果 fruit, was earlier written as 果 or 果 , which are pictures of fruit on a tree.

Write the characters

城 chéng *town*	谢 xiè *to thank*	都 dōu *all*	炒 chǎo *to stir-fry*	米 mǐ *uncooked rice*
客 kè *guest*	气 qì *air*	馆 guǎn *building*	得 de *[degree, result of]*	常 cháng *often*
因 yīn *cause*	为 wèi *for*	所 suǒ *so; place*	平 píng *flat*	茶 chá *tea*

everyoneloveswangli•everyoneloveswangli•everyoneloveswangli•everyoneloveswangli•every

做 得 很 好

林朋喜欢吃炒饭，可是学校不卖炒饭。
xuéxiào
他中午在学校常常吃三明治、汉堡包和热狗。
sānmíngzhì   hànbǎobāo   règǒu
上星期四中午吃饭时，林朋说他很想吃炒饭。

王利说他会做炒饭，他可以早上
在家里做，中午请林朋吃。

星期五早上，因为王利很晚
起床，所以他在学校旁边的中国
qǐchuáng   xuéxiào pángbiān
饭馆买了炒饭，中午请林朋吃。

现在林朋常常说："王利炒饭做
得很好。"

About Pinyin and characters

Neutral Tone

Characters that usually appear at the end of a sentence and carry an exclamation or question voice are always pronounced in neutral tone, eg. 吗 ma, 呢 ne, 吧 ba, 啊 a, etc. Whereas some characters may have their original tone which changes into neutral tone in some circumstances, eg.

When used as a suffix with no strong meaning –
左边 zuǒbian (biān), 前面 qiánmian (miàn), 早上 zǎoshang (shàng), 桌子 zhuōzi (zǐ)

When repeatedly used in a word –
爸爸 bàba, 哥哥 gēge, 叔叔 shūshu, 太太 tàitai

When repeating the meaning of, or carrying a softer meaning than its preceding character in a word –
衣服 yīfu (fú), 耳朵 ěrduo (duǒ), 眼睛 yǎnjing (jīng), 凉快 liángkuai (kuài)

Something to know

❀ Food balance

The Chinese believe that food contains the nature of yīn 阴 or yáng 阳, that is, having *the properties of cooling or warming.* Cooling foods such as bean curd, watermelon, celery and green tea often contain less calories while warming foods such as cherries, ginger, chilli, meat and black tea often contain more calories. Cooking methods can alter the cooling or warming nature of food. For example, deep-fried foods tend to be warming and pickled foods are cooling. A balance of cooling and warming foods is important in the Chinese diet.

❀ Bean curd in Chinese diet

Bean curd, dòufu 豆腐, which is made from soybeans and is high in protein, is a favourite of most Chinese. Not having much flavour in itself, dòufu combines well with almost any ingredients to produce a great variety of tastes. It can be steamed, boiled, deep-fried, or shallow-fried. Dòufu is used in simple cooking for the daily family meal and can also be a luxurious dish for a special occasion. The popular hot and spicy dish mápó-dòufu 麻婆豆腐 is said to have been invented by a pockmark-faced widow who ran a little restaurant for a living. The term mápó means pockmark-faced old woman.

Family meal

The family meal is generally simpler than that at a restaurant. The staple food is rice in southern China and wheat products in northern China. Although meals vary from place to place and from day to day, a typical breakfast may consist of rice porridge with eggs and pickled vegetables, or soybean milk with sesame seed cakes, shāobǐng 烧饼, and deep-fried dough sticks, yóutiáo 油条. For lunch, it could be a bowl of noodle soup and for dinner, rice or steamed buns with vegetables, soup and meat or fish.

The Chinese habitually have their rice and other dishes first and the soup last. However, most Chinese restaurants overseas have adopted the Western style and serve the soup at the beginning of the meal.

When guests are invited for a meal at home, the Chinese often use modest words at the table. Wǒ tàitai bú huì zuò cài 我太太不会做菜, Cài zuò de bù hǎo 菜做得不好, or Méi shénme cài 没什么菜, are commonly used although there may be a full table of their best cooking.

Addressing friends' parents

It is considered rude to call older people by their names in Chinese society. There are polite forms of address which vary from place to place. The most common forms used by children to address their friends' parents or parents' friends are shūshu 叔叔 and āyí 阿姨. Shūshu is a term used for the younger brothers of the father, but is used here to address males of one's parents' generation, while āyí is used for females. In some areas, bóbo 伯伯, a term for the father's older brother, and bómǔ 伯母, a term for his wife, are used if the person looks obviously much older than one's parents. In Taiwan and in some southern areas, the surname followed by māma 妈妈 is often used for married females.

Would you like a cup of coffee?

During a formal visit, if the host asks the guest: Would you like a cup of coffee? Yào bú yào hē bēi kāfēi? 要不要喝杯咖啡? the reply will normally be no, búyào 不要, even if the guest is thirsty. Chinese regard saying I would love to, wǒ yào 我要, as impolite. Saying no means that the guest does not want to cause the host too much trouble. Chinese drink tea at home rather than coffee. Normally, the host will offer the guest some tea, a cold drink, or fruit without asking.

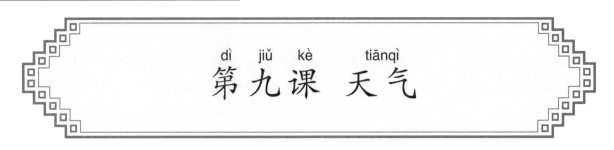

dì jiǔ kè   tiānqì
第九课 天气

1 **What's the weather like today?**

tiānqì
今天天气怎么样？

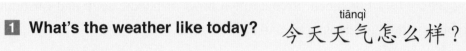

tiānqì
今天天气很好。

fēng
今天风很大。

xiàyǔ
今天下雨。

xiàxuě
今天下雪。

rè
今天很热。

lěng
今天很冷。

liángkuai
今天很凉快。

2 Beijing's weather

Běijīng chūntiān
北京的春天怎么样？

fēngshā
北京的春天风沙很大。

xiàtiān
北京的夏天热吗？

yòu
又热，又常下雨。

qiūtiān
北京的秋天怎么样？

liángkuai
北京的秋天很凉快。

dōngtiān
北京的冬天冷吗？

很冷，可是不常下雪。

3 Weather forecast

天气预报
yùbào

昨天：阴雨
yīnyǔ

最高气温摄氏二十七度，最低二十四度。
zuìgāo qìwēn shèshì dù zuìdī dù

今天：多云
yún

最高气温三十二度，最低二十六度。
zuìgāo qìwēn dù zuìdī

明天：晴，有雷阵雨
qíng léizhènyǔ

最高气温三十八度，最低十九度。

4 **It's going to rain**

Learn the sentences

✳ **Inquiring about the weather**

To ask What's the weather like today? say 今天天气怎么样？ Jīntiān tiānqì zěnmeyàng?
To answer, state the condition, such as It's raining today, say 今天下雨。Jīntiān xiàyǔ. and
It is cold today, say 今天很冷。 Jīntiān hěn lěng.

今天天气怎么样？	今天下雨。
	今天下雪。
昨天天气怎么样？	昨天风很大。
	昨天天气很好。
明天天气怎么样？	明天会很冷。
	明天会很热。

✳ **Use of 又 yòu**

又 yòu can be used repeatedly to display two conditions or two actions happening at one
time or in one go, e.g. 又 ... ... 又 ... ... yòu... yòu....

北京的夏天又热，又常下雨。

这儿的冬天又冷，又常下雪。

这苹果又贵，又不好吃。

那件衣服又漂亮，又便宜。

✳ **Asking about the season**

怎么样 zěnmeyàng, how about or what about, is a simple way to ask about the situation or condition of something. We have learnt to use it to ask about clothing, the weather and here, about the seasons.

北京的春天怎么样？	北京的春天风沙(fēngshā)很大。
北京的夏天怎么样？	北京的夏天很热。
这儿的秋天怎么样？	这儿的秋天很漂亮(piàoliang)。
那儿的冬天怎么样？	那儿的冬天会下雪。

✳ **Use of 死了 sǐ le**

死 sǐ, literally death or die, can be used orally as an adverb to describe an extreme situation.

今天热死(sǐ)了。
昨天冷死了。
我饿死了；我们去吃点儿东西(dōngxi)吧！
我渴死了；我们去喝点儿东西吧！

✳ **Use of 就 jiù**

就 jiù has many ways of usage. It is used here to indicate a consequence from a condition previously stated. It often follows 那 nà or 那么 nàme, meaning then or therefore.

今天冷死(sǐ)了。	那就(jiù)多穿点儿衣服吧！
下午会下雨。	那就带(dài)雨衣吧！
那件衣服很便宜。	那就买吧！
下雨了。	那就不要去打球了！

✳ **Use of 会 huì to indicate the future**

The word 会 huì is often used to describe something which is going to or likely to happen in the future. For example, to say It's going to rain tomorrow, say 明天会下雨。 Míngtiān huì xiàyǔ.

明天天气怎么样？	明天会下雨。
后天天气怎么样？	后天会很冷。
你看明天会下雨吗？	我看不会吧！
妈妈下午会回来吗？	会，她下午三点回来。
你明天会去上学吗？	不会，明天是星期六。

 New words and expressions

天气	tiānqì	weather tiān- sky, day; qì- air, manner
风	fēng	wind

下雨	xiàyǔ	to rain xià- (of rain or snow) to fall, down; yǔ- rain
下雪	xiàxuě	to snow xià- (of rain or snow) to fall, down; xuě- snow
热	rè	hot
冷	lěng	cold
凉快	liángkuai	cool and pleasant liáng- cool; kuài- fast, soon
北京	Běijīng	the capital city of China běi- north; jīng- capital
春天	chūntiān	spring chūn- spring; tiān- sky, day
风沙	fēngshā	dust storm fēng- wind; shā- sand
夏天	xiàtiān	summer xià- summer; tiān- sky, day
又... 又...	yòu... yòu...	[indicating more than one condition] and yòu- again
秋天	qiūtiān	autumn qiū- autumn, fall; tiān- sky, day
冬天	dōngtiān	winter dōng- winter; tiān- sky, day
天气预报	tiānqì yùbào	weather forecast tiānqì- weather; yùbào- forecast
阴雨	yīnyǔ	overcast and rainy
最高	zuìgāo	highest zuì- the most; gāo- high
气温	qìwēn	temperature qì- air; wēn- warm
摄氏	shèshì	centigrade (Fahrenheit- 华氏 Huáshì)
度	dù	degree (temperature)
最低	zuìdī	lowest zuì- the most; dī- low
云	yún	cloud (cloudy- 多云 duōyún)
晴	qíng	fine, sunny (fine day, sunny day- 晴天 qíngtiān)
雷阵雨	léizhènyǔ	thunder shower léi- thunder; zhènyǔ- shower
死	sǐ	deathly; dead; to die
就	jiù	[indicating a consequence] therefore, then, details see p. 100
哇	wā	wow [exclamation]
会	huì	1. will; 2. be able to, can
带	dài	to bring, to take
雨衣	yǔyī	raincoat yǔ- rain; yī- clothes
雨伞	yǔsǎn	umbrella yǔ- rain; sǎn- umbrella
拿	ná	to take, to bring (by hand); hold

Laundry day

今天真热！最高气温三十六度。

今天是很热！

今天热死了！最高气温三十八度。

今天是热死了！

因为天气预报说今天会下雨，所以我没洗衣服。

可是今天没下雨。

因为天气预报说今天会有雷阵雨，所以我也没洗衣服。

可是今天没有雷阵雨。

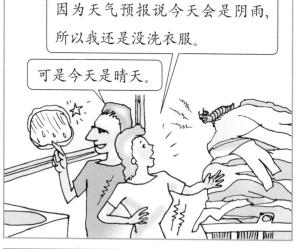

因为天气预报说今天会是阴雨，所以我还是没洗衣服。

可是今天是晴天。

太好了！天气预报说今天会是晴天。我可以洗衣服了！

洗，今天洗衣服！

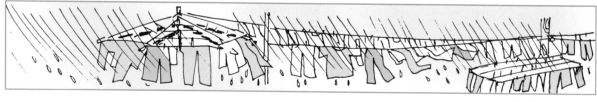

Write the characters

风	雨	雪	热	冷
fēng *wind*	yǔ *rain*	xuě *snow*	rè *hot*	lěng *cold*
凉	北	京	春	夏
liáng *cool*	běi *north*	jīng *capital*	chūn *spring*	xià *summer*
秋	冬	阴	最	晴
qiū *autumn, fall*	dōng *winter*	yīn *cloudy*	zuì *the most*	qíng *sunny, fine*

·everyoneloveswangli·everyoneloveswangli·everyoneloveswangli·everyoneloveswangli·everyone

别 去 了
bié

　　早上林朋到王利家，他们要
一块儿去打网球。今天很热，上
午的气温是摄氏三十八度。王利
说："太热了，别去打网球了。我
看，我们上午在家看电视，下午去
游泳。"

　　吃午饭时，电视的天气预报说下
午会有雷阵雨，风很大，雨也很大。
王利说："我看，别去游泳了。我
们再看电视吧！"

Something to know

✿ Climate in China

Due to the vastness of the country, the weather in China varies dramatically from region to region. The country covers a total area of approximately 9.6 million square kilometres with mountains in the west and plains in the east. The climate ranges from frigid in the north to tropical in the south. The average annual rainfall is 1500 mm in the humid southeast and only 50 mm in the arid northwest. The hottest area in summer is in Turpan, Tǔlǔfān 吐鲁番, in Xīnjiāng 新疆 where the average daytime temperature in July exceeds 40°C. The coldest area is in the Hǎilā'ěr 海拉尔 district in Inner Mongolia, Nèi Měnggǔ 内蒙古, where the average temperature in January is -27.7°C. Hēilóngjiāng 黑龙江 province is entirely without summer, and Hǎinán Island 海南岛 is virtually without winter. In the Huáihé 淮河 basin, the four seasons are clearly defined, while in Kūnmíng 昆明, it is spring-like all year round.

✿ Key tourist spots in China

With a vast land and a long history, China's physical and cultural attractions are plentiful. Tourists are fascinated by the beautiful scenery of the ancient sacred mountains: Tàishān 泰山 in Shāndōng 山东 province and Huàshān 华山 in Shǎnxī 陕西 province. Visitors to Tàishān can climb up 7000 steps to its peak to admire the beauty of nature. West Lake, Xīhú 西湖, in Hángzhōu 杭州 was a favourite topic for ancient poets and still displays poetic beauty. The limestone pinnacles in Guìlín 桂林 and the Stone Forest, Shílín 石林, in Yúnnán 云南 province, exhibit the fantastic craft of nature.

The Buddhist murals and statues in the caves of Dūnhuáng 敦煌 and Yúngāng 云冈, and the giant 71-metre high Buddha at the hill of Lèshān 乐山 are masterpieces of human endeavour. The unearthed terracotta warriors in Xī'ān 西安 are representative of the empire of Qín Shǐhuáng 秦始皇.

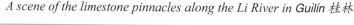

A scene of the limestone pinnacles along the Li River in Guìlín 桂林

The giant Buddha in Lèshān 乐山

Chángchéng 长城, the Great Wall

In Běijīng 北京, the renovated section of the Great Wall, Chángchéng 长城, in Bādálǐng 八达岭 tells of the history of Chinese expansion. The Forbidden City, Zǐjìnchéng 紫禁城, presents the magnificence of the ancient palace, and Fragrance Hill, Xiāngshān 香山, displays its splendid red foliage in autumn.

❋ Key tourist spots in Taiwan

An island smaller than Tasmania with its highest mountain at 3950 metres provides Taiwan with spectacular scenery. Taroko Gorge, Tàilǔgé 太鲁阁, at the entrance of the Cross-island Highway, Héngguàn Gōnglù 横贯公路, features a magnificent marble gorge; Ali mountain, Ālǐshān 阿里山, displays a turbulent sea of clouds and a beautiful sunrise; The National Chungshan Museum, Zhōngshān Bówùyuàn 中山博物院 (or briefly called Gùgōng 故宫) shows the abundant treasures of Chinese culture.

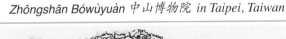

Zhōngshān Bówùyuàn 中山博物院 in Taipei, Taiwan

第十课 复习（二）
dì shí kè fùxí èr

1 A diary

二〇〇八年八月六日，星期六，雨天

今天又冷又下雨。早上的气温是摄氏 (qìwēn) (shèshì)

七度 (dù)。因为八月十六日是小明的生日，所以我十二点

要和大伟 (Dàwěi) 一起去百货商店 (bǎihuò shāngdiàn) 买东西 (dōngxi) 给他。我喜欢下雨天

骑车 (qíchē)，也喜欢穿雨衣骑车。十一点半，我就骑车去百

货商店。

我在百货商店 (bǎihuò shāngdiàn) 等大伟。十二点四十五分了，可是

大伟还没来。我打电话给他。他说："买东西 (dōngxi) 给小明？

不是今天！是下个星期六。"

我冷死 (sǐ) 了，也饿死了。我就 (jiù) 在百货商店买了一件

黄色的大外套 (wàitào)，又自己 (yòu zìjǐ) 一个人在商

店旁边 (pángbiān) 的中国饭馆吃午饭。

2 Language functions

[6] Asking the price

这手机多少钱？　Zhè shǒujī duōshǎo qián?

一百九十五块。　Yìbǎi jiǔshíwǔ kuài.

Asking how things are sold

苹果怎么卖？　Píngguǒ zěnme mài?

香蕉一斤多少钱？　Xiāngjiāo yì jīn duōshǎo qián?

菠萝一个多少钱？　Bōluó yí gè duōshǎo qián?

Expressing the degree of an opinion

这荔枝太贵了。　Zhè lìzhī tài guì le.

这西瓜一点儿都不贵。　Zhè xīguā yìdiǎnr dōu bú guì.

Making comparisons

这件衣服很贵。　Zhè jiàn yīfu hěn guì.

那件衣服便宜点儿。　Nà jiàn yīfu piányi diǎnr.

那条裤子更便宜。　Nà tiáo kùzi gèng piányi.

Asking for another option

这件太大了，有没有小点儿的？　Zhè jiàn tài dà le, yǒu méiyǒu xiǎo diǎnr de?

这件还是大，有没有更小的？　Zhè jiàn háishi dà, yǒu méiyǒu gèng xiǎo de?

[7] Asking if someone is home

请问你爸爸在家吗？　Qǐngwèn nǐ bàba zài jiā ma?

他在。我去叫他。　Tā zài. Wǒ qù jiào tā.

他不在。您是哪位？　Tā bú zài. Nín shì nǎ wèi?

Asking when someone is coming back

你妈妈什么时候回来？　Nǐ māma shénme shíhou huílái?

她下午三点左右回来。　Tā xiàwǔ sān diǎn zuǒyòu huílái.

Asking who is speaking on the telephone

您是哪位？　Nín shì nǎ wèi?

我是黄阿姨。　Wǒ shì Huáng āyí.

Asking if someone has come back

你哥哥回来了吗？　Nǐ gēge huílái le ma?

他回来了。　Tā huílái le.

他还没回来。　Tā hái méi huílái.

Asking someone's telephone number

你的电话号码是多少？　Nǐ de diànhuà hàomǎ shì duōshǎo?

是五四三二六七八九。　Shì wǔ sì sān èr liù qī bā jiǔ.

Asking someone who he/she is looking for

您找谁？　Nín zhǎo shéi?

我找你姐姐。她在吗？　Wǒ zhǎo nǐ jiějie. Tā zài ma?

Asking if someone is available

你今天下午有空吗？　Nǐ jīntiān xiàwǔ yǒu kòng ma?

我有空。有什么事吗？　Wǒ yǒu kòng. Yǒu shénme shì ma?

我下午没空。　Wǒ xiàwǔ méi kòng.

Seeking agreement

我明天打电话给你，可以吗？ Wǒ míngtiān dǎ diànhuà gěi nǐ, kěyǐ ma?

行，我等你的电话。 Xíng, wǒ děng nǐ de diànhuà.

不行，我明天不在家。 Bù xíng, wǒ míngtiān bú zài jiā.

[8] Ordering food

您点什么菜？ Nín diǎn shénme cài?

来一盘麻婆豆腐和一盘青菜。 Lái yì pán mápó-dòufu hé yì pán qīngcài.

Offering a choice

您要吃米饭还是炒饭？ Nín yào chī mǐfàn háishi chǎofàn?

我吃炒饭。 Wǒ chī chǎofàn.

Expressing usually or often

他们常去中国饭馆吃饭。 Tāmen cháng qù Zhōngguó fànguǎn chīfàn.

我们不常去饭馆吃饭。 Wǒmen bù cháng qù fànguǎn chīfàn.

我们平常都吃中国菜。 Wǒmen píngcháng dōu chī Zhōngguó cài.

Explaining cause

因为下雨，所以弟弟不去上学。 Yīnwèi xiàyǔ, suǒyǐ dìdi bú qù shàngxué.

因为今天衣服打折，所以我买了三件。

Yīnwèi jīntiān yīfu dǎzhé, suǒyǐ wǒ mǎi le sān jiàn.

Expressions used by the host

别客气。– 我不客气。 Bié kèqi. – Wǒ bú kèqi.

你自己来。– 好，我自己来。 Nǐ zìjǐ lái. – Hǎo, wǒ zìjǐ lái.

今天没什么菜。– 您太客气了。 Jīntiān méi shénme cài. – Nín tài kèqi le.

多吃点儿。– 我吃很多了。 Duō chī diǎnr. – Wǒ chī hěn duō le.

[9] Inquiring about the weather

今天天气怎么样？ Jīntiān tiānqì zěnmeyàng?

今天天气很好。 Jīntiān tiānqì hěn hǎo.

Use of "又 yòu"

昨天又冷，又下雨。 Zuótiān yòu lěng, yòu xiàyǔ.

那件衣服又贵，又不好看。 Nà jiàn yīfu yòu guì, yòu bù hǎokàn.

Asking about the season

这儿的春天怎么样？ Zhèr de chūntiān zěnmeyàng?

这儿的春天常下雨。 Zhèr de chūntiān cháng xiàyǔ.

Use of "死了 sǐ le"

今天热死了。 Jīntiān rè sǐ le.

我饿死了。你饿不饿？ Wǒ è sǐ le. Nǐ è bú è?

Use of "就 jiù"

衣服便宜，那就买吧。 Yīfu piányi, nà jiù mǎi ba.

下雨了，那就不要去打球了。 Xiàyǔ le, nà jiù bú yào qù dǎqiú le.

Use of "会 huì" to indicate the future

明天会下雨。 Míngtiān huì xiàyǔ.

你妈妈下午会回来吗？ Nǐ māma xiàwǔ huì huílái ma?

会，她三点左右回来。 Huì, tā sān diǎn zuǒyòu huílái.

Appendix 1

WORDS AND EXPRESSIONS
Chinese-English

m.w.- measure word

	Simplified	Pinyin	English	Traditional	Lesson
A	阿姨	āyí	used to address women of mother's age; (in southern regions) mother's sister	阿姨	8
	唉	ài	(a sigh)	唉	4
B	白饭	báifàn	(in Taiwan) plain rice	白飯	8
	白色	báisè	white	白色	4
	百货商店	bǎihuò shāngdiàn	department store	百貨商店	4
	半	bàn	half	半	2
	北京	Běijīng	the capital city of China	北京	9
	本	běn	[*m.w.* - book, magazine etc]	本	6
	别	bié	don't, do not	別	8
	菠萝	bōluó	pineapple, also called 凤梨 fènglí	菠蘿／鳳梨	6
	不错	búcuò	pretty good, not bad	不錯	8
C	菜单	càidān	menu	菜單	8
	草莓	cǎoméi	strawberry	草莓	6
	厕所	cèsuǒ	toilet, lavatory	廁所	3
	茶	chá	tea	茶	2
	长	cháng	long	長	4
	常	cháng	often, also said 常常 cháng cháng	常	8
	唱歌	chànggē	to sing, singing	唱歌	2
	炒	chǎo	to stir-fry	炒	8
	炒饭	chǎofàn	fried rice	炒飯	8
	车	chē	car, vehicle	車	3
	车库	chēkù	garage	車庫	3
	衬衫	chènshān	shirt	襯衫	4
	出去	chūqù	to go out	出去	7
	厨房	chúfáng	kitchen	廚房	3
	穿	chuān	to wear (clothes, shoes or socks)	穿	4
	床	chuáng	bed	床	3
	春天	chūntiān	spring	春天	9
	错	cuò	wrong, incorrect	錯	1
D	打	dǎ	to dial (telephone); to play (ball game, tai chi etc)	打	2
	打折	dǎzhé	discount	打折	4

Simplified	Pinyin	English	Traditional	Lesson
带	dài	to bring, to take	帶	9
蛋糕	dàngāo	cake	蛋糕	1
等	děng	to wait	等	7
地图	dìtú	map	地圖	6
点	diǎn	o'clock; dot;	點	2
		to point		8
点菜	diǎncài	to order dishes from a menu	點菜	8
点儿	diǎnr	a little, short for 一点儿	點兒	6
电冰箱	diànbīngxiāng	refrigerator	電冰箱	3
电话	diànhuà	telephone	電話	2
电脑	diànnǎo	computer	電腦	3
电视	diànshì	television	電視	3
电视机	diànshìjī	television set	電視機	3
冬天	dōngtiān	winter	冬天	9
都	dōu	all	都	3
度	dù	degree (temperature)	度	9
对	duì	right, correct	對	1
对了	duìle	by the way	對了	8
多	duō	much, many	多	4
多少	duōshǎo	how much, how many	多少	6
多云	duōyún	cloudy	多雲	9
F 饭馆	fànguǎn	restaurant	飯館	8
饭厅	fàntīng	dining room	飯廳	3
房间	fángjiān	room, bedroom	房間	3
房子	fángzi	house	房子	3
放	fàng	to put; to let off, to let go	放	8
放学	fàngxué	to finish classes	放學	2
非常	fēicháng	extremely	非常	6
肥	féi	loose-fitting (clothing); fat	肥	4
分	fēn	minute;	分	2
		one-cent unit		6
风	fēng	wind	風	9
风沙	fēngshā	dust storm	風沙	9
服装店	fúzhuāngdiàn	clothes shop	服裝店	6
G 该	gāi	should	該	4
刚	gāng	just	剛	7
给	gěi	to give	給	6
更	gèng	even, even more	更	6
功课	gōngkè	school work, homework	功課	2
公斤	gōngjīn	kilogram	公斤	6
公寓	gōngyù	apartment	公寓	3

Simplified	Pinyin	English	Traditional	Lesson
古老肉	gǔlǎoròu	sweet and sour pork	咕咾肉	8
光临	guānglín	[polite form] gracious presence (of guests)	光臨	8
贵	guì	expensive, dear	貴	6
H 还	hái	also, still	還	3
还是	háishi	1. still;	還是	6
		2. or		8
好了好了	hǎo le hǎo le	that's enough (to stop someone from doing something)	好了好了	1
好看	hǎokàn	good-looking	好看	4
号	hào	date; number	號	1
号码	hàomǎ	number	號碼	7
黑色	hēisè	black	黑色	4
红色	hóngsè	red	紅色	4
后面	hòumian	behind	後面	3
后年	hòunián	the year after next	後年	1
后天	hòutiān	the day after tomorrow	後天	1
华氏	Huáshì	Fahrenheit	華氏	9
欢迎	huānyíng	welcome	歡迎	8
黄	huáng; Huáng	yellow; a family name	黃	4
黄色	huángsè	yellow	黃色	4
灰色	huīsè	grey	灰色	4
回来	huílái	to come back, to return	回來	7
会	huì	1. will; 2. be able to, can	會	9
J 家人	jiārén	family member	家人	3
间	jiān	[m.w. - room]	間	3
件	jiàn	[m.w. - clothing or affair]	件	4
角	jiǎo	[formal] 10-cent unit	角	6
接	jiē	1. to meet, to pick (someone) up;	接	7
		2. to answer the telephone		
斤	jīn	a unit of weight (= 0.5 kilograms)	斤	6
今年	jīnnián	this year	今年	1
今天	jīntiān	today	今天	1
进	jìn	to enter	進	8
就	jiù	[indicating a consequence] therefore, then	就	9
橘子	júzi	mandarin, tangerine	橘子	6
K 咖啡色	kāfēisè	brown	咖啡色	7
看	kàn	to read, to see, to watch	看	2
可以	kěyǐ	can, may	可以	7
刻	kè	a quarter (of an hour)	刻	2
客气	kèqi	courteous	客氣	8

Simplified	Pinyin	English	Traditional	Lesson
客厅	kètīng	living room, lounge	客廳	3
空	kòng	free time, spare time	空	7
裤子	kùzi	trousers, pants	褲子	4
块	kuài	[oral] monetary unit for dollar	塊	6
快	kuài	soon; fast	快	2
快乐	kuàilè	happy	快樂	1
宽	kuān	(in Taiwan) loose-fitting (clothing)	寬	4

L 来	lái	to come	來	1
来……	lái...	to give (me/us)... (used when ordering food)	來……	8
蓝色	lánsè	blue	藍色	4
了	le	[grammatical word] details see p. 24	了	2
雷阵雨	léizhènyǔ	thunder shower	雷陣雨	9
冷	lěng	cold	冷	9
里面	lǐmian	inside	裡面	3
荔枝	lìzhī	lychee	荔枝	6
连衣裙	liányīqún	woman's dress	連衣裙	4
凉快	liángkuai	cool and pleasant	涼快	9
零，〇	líng	zero	零	1
龙眼	lóngyǎn	longan	龍眼	6
楼	lóu	storeyed building	樓	3
楼房	lóufáng	multi-storey building	樓房	3
楼上	lóushàng	upstairs	樓上	3
楼下	lóuxià	downstairs	樓下	3
绿色	lùsè	green	綠色	4

M 麻婆豆腐	mápó-dòufu	name of a hot and spicy bean curd dish	麻婆豆腐	8
马上	mǎshàng	right away	馬上	7
买	mǎi	to buy	買	4
卖	mài	to sell	賣	6
毛	máo	[oral] 10-cent unit; fur	毛	6, 4
毛衣	máoyī	sweater	毛衣	4
没问题	méi wèntí	no problems	沒問題	8
米饭	mǐfàn	plain rice	米飯	8
棉袄	mián'ǎo	cotton-padded coat	棉襖	4
秒	miǎo	second (time)	秒	2
明年	míngnián	next year	明年	1
明天	míngtiān	tomorrow	明天	1

N 拿	ná	take, bring (by hand); hold	拿	9
哪儿	nǎr	[oral] where	哪兒	3
哪位	nǎ/něi wèi	which one (person)	哪位	7
那	nà	then, in that case, short for 那么 nàme	那	7

Simplified	Pinyin	English	Traditional	Lesson
年	nián	year	年	1
您	nín	[polite form] you	您	6
O 哦	ò	[to indicate realization] oh	哦	1
P 盘	pán	[m.w. - dish] plate	盤	8
便宜	piányi	cheap, inexpensive	便宜	6
旁边	pángbiān	side	旁邊	8
漂亮	piàoliang	pretty	漂亮	4
平常	píngcháng	usually	平常	8
平房	píngfáng	single-storey house	平房	3
苹果	píngguǒ	apple	蘋果	6
葡萄	pútáo	grapes	葡萄	6
Q 旗袍	qípáo	close-fitting dress with a high neck and slit skirt	旗袍	4
起床	qǐchuáng	to get up, to get out of bed	起床	2
起来	qǐlai	[indicating impressions]	起來	4
汽水	qìshuǐ	soft drink, soda pop	汽水	8
气温	qìwēn	temperature	氣溫	9
钱	qián	money	錢	6
前面	qiánmian	front	前面	3
前年	qiánnián	the year before last	前年	1
前天	qiántiān	the day before yesterday	前天	1
青菜	qīngcài	green vegetable	青菜	8
晴	qíng	sunny, fine	晴	9
晴天	qíngtiān	fine day, sunny day	晴天	9
请	qǐng	to invite; please	請	1
请进	qǐng jìn	come in please	請進	8
请坐	qǐng zuò	sit down please	請坐	8
秋天	qiūtiān	autumn	秋天	9
去年	qùnián	last year	去年	1
裙子	qúnzi	skirt	裙子	4
R 热	rè	hot	熱	9
日	rì	day; sun	日	1
S 沙发	shāfā	sofa (transliteration of sofa)	沙發	3
商店	shāngdiàn	shop	商店	6
上	shàng	1. up, above; 2. to go to	上	8
上个星期	shàng gè xīngqī	last week	上個星期	1
上个月	shàng gè yuè	last month	上個月	1
上面	shàngmian	on top of, above	上面	3
上午	shàngwǔ	morning	上午	2

Simplified	Pinyin	English	Traditional	Lesson
上学	shàngxué	to go to school	上學	2
摄氏	shèshì	centigrade	攝氏	9
生	shēng	to be born, to give birth to; pupil	生	1
生日	shēngrì	birthday	生日	1
狮子头	shīzitóu	a dish of fried meatballs	獅子頭	8
… … 时	… shí	when...	時	7
时候	shíhou	time, moment	時候	1
时髦	shímáo	fashion, fashionable	時髦	4
事	shì	matter, thing, business	事	7
市场	shìchǎng	market	市場	6
手机	shǒujī	mobile phone	手機	3
瘦	shòu	tight-fitting (clothing); thin	瘦	4
书房	shūfáng	study	書房	3
舒服	shūfu	comfortable	舒服	4
叔叔	shūshu	father's younger brother; also used to address men of father's age	叔叔	7
水果	shuǐguǒ	fruit	水果	6
睡觉	shuìjiào	to sleep	睡覺	2
死	sǐ	deathly; dead; to die	死	9
酸	suān	sour	酸	6
酸辣汤	suānlàtāng	hot and sour soup	酸辣湯	8
所以	suǒyǐ	therefore	所以	8

	Simplified	Pinyin	English	Traditional	Lesson
T	T恤衫	T xùshān	T-shirt	T恤衫	4
	太	tài	too, excessively	太	4
	太极拳	tàijíquán	tai chi	太極拳	3
	太太	tàitai	Mrs; (in Taiwan) wife	太太	4
	汤	tāng	soup	湯	8
	天气	tiānqì	weather	天氣	9
	天气预报	tiānqì yùbào	weather forecast	天氣預報	9
	甜	tián	sweet	甜	6
	条	tiáo	[m.w. - trousers, shorts, skirt etc]	條	4
	跳舞	tiàowǔ	to dance	跳舞	2
	听	tīng	to listen, to hear	聽	2
	挺	tǐng	[oral] very	挺	4

	Simplified	Pinyin	English	Traditional	Lesson
W	哇	wā	wow [exclamation]	哇	9
	外面	wàimian	outside	外面	3
	外套	wàitào	coat	外套	4
	碗	wǎn	[m.w. - rice or soup] bowl	碗	8
	晚	wǎn	late, evening	晚	3
	晚饭	wǎnfàn	dinner	晚飯	2
	晚上	wǎnshang	evening, night	晚上	2